CORONEL
AND
FALKLAND

CORONEL
AND
FALKLAND

BARRIE PITT

CASSELL&CO

For Toni

Cassell Military Paperbacks

Cassell & Co
Wellington House, 125 Strand
London WC2R 0BB

First published by Cassell 1960
This Cassell Military Paperbacks edition 2002

British Library Cataloguing-in-Publication Data
A catalogue record for this book is available from the
British Library

ISBN 0-304-36160-7

Printed and bound in Great Britain by
Cox & Wyman Ltd., Reading, Berks.

AUTHOR'S NOTE

Such a book as this cannot be written without the help and co-operation of a large number of people. Commander M. G. Saunders and Mr H. C. Beaumont of the Admiralty Historical Section have guided me in the use of material from published German sources, and from the numerous survivors of the battles I would like especially to thank Captain T. H. Back and also to mention the late Mr J. R. Warburton, who lent me his private letters and diaries and spared me much of his time—time, alas, of which he knew quite well he had little left.

Mr J. W. Stock too, has given me much invaluable advice and the benefit of his knowledge of naval lore and history—not to speak of the use I made of his private library in Wiltshire.

To these and many others, I tender my grateful thanks, for they provided much factual material and pointed the way to other sources of information.

But for the opinions expressed in this book, and especially for the reconstruction of events which I believe led Admiral Graf von Spee to attack the Falkland Islands, I alone am responsible. The known facts are few and are restricted to the positions and movements of the East Asiatic Squadron at certain times, the weather conditions and the various signals and instructions which appear in the Appendix. Other interpretations than mine have been placed upon these facts.

One of these other interpretations might encompass the truth —and so might this.

BARRIE PITT

ACKNOWLEDGEMENTS

From the abundance of literature covering, or mentioning, the battles of Coronel and the Falkland Islands, I would like to acknowledge particularly my debt to the following:

The Battle Cruisers at the Action of the Falkland Islands, Rudolph Verner, John Bale, Sons & Danielsson.

The Battle of the Falkland Islands, H. Spencer-Cooper, Cassell.

Before Jutland, Hans Pochhammer, Jarrolds.

Coronel and After, Lloyd Hirst, Peter Davies.

Coronel and the Falklands, John Irving, A. M. Philpot.

Der Krieg zur Zee, Erich Raeder, E. S. Mittler & Son.

Naval Operations of the Great War, Vol. I, Sir Julian Corbett, Longmans Green.

Naval Review, Vol. VIII, No. 1.

Whispers from the Fleet, Sir Christopher Cradock.

The World Crisis, Winston S. Churchill, Thornton Butterworth (Odhams Press).

ILLUSTRATIONS

Rear-Admiral Sir Christopher Cradock, K.C.V.O., C.B., M.V.O.*

H.M.S. *Glasgow**

A.M.C. *Otranto**

H.M.S. *Good Hope**

H.M.S. *Monmouth**

H.M.S. *Canopus**

Winston Churchill and Admiral Lord Fisher (*Radio Times Hulton Picture Library*)

Sinking the tender *Titania* (*from Hans Pochhammer's* Before Jutland)

Scharnhorst, Gneisenau and *Nürnberg* leaving Valparaiso Bay, 4 November 1914*

Vice-Admiral Graf von Spee (*from Hans Pochhammer's* Before Jutland)

S.M.S. *Scharnhorst**

Vice-Admiral Sir Frederick Doveton Sturdee, K.C.B., C.M.G., C.V.O. (*from* The Times History of the Great War)

H.M.S. *Invincible**

The guns of *Inflexible*

H.M.S. *Inflexible**

H.M.S. *Bristol**

H.M.S. *Carnarvon**

H.M.S. *Cornwall**

H.M.S. *Kent**

'Enemy approaching Port William' (*from the water-colour by Lieut-Commander Verner*)

'Last rounds falling about *Scharnhorst*' (*from the water-colour by Lieut-Commander Verner*)

Survivors from *Gneisenau* (*from Hans Pochhammer's* Before Jutland)

S.M.S. *Dresden**

*Crown Copyright Photograph, Imperial War Museum

MAPS

	Page
The Battle of Coronel, 1 Nov.	10
The Routes to the Falkland Is., 1 Nov.–8 Dec.	86
Port Stanley Harbour, Morning, 8 Dec.	104
Battle-Cruiser Action, 8 Dec.	116
The Battle of the Falkland Is., 8 Dec.	140

INTRODUCTION

THE outbreak of war in August 1914 did not catch the Armed Services of the Crown in half the state of anxiety and unpreparedness that many critics would have us believe. The Royal Navy, for instance, despite the limitations imposed by financial and political factors of the early 1900s, was quite capable of carrying out the major portion of its initial duties—at any rate in Home Waters— and indeed did so with estimable efficiency and speed. Within a matter of days the Grand Fleet had established a control over the northern entrance to the North Sea through which the only enemy surface vessels ever to pass were the occasional solitary (and extremely fortunate) commerce raider; troop convoys crossed the Channel to the battle areas in large numbers and apparently complete safety, the German battle-cruiser *Goeben* and her consort *Breslau* in the Mediterranean, if not caught and sunk, were at least chased away from the danger areas and up into the Bosphorus, and from all the rest of the wide seas which covered the globe, the German mercantile and naval flags virtually disappeared.

But not entirely.

In those early years of the century, Germany had many oversea possessions and protectorates, many centres of business interest. Units of the Imperial German Navy therefore kept watch and patrol in waters far from the Fatherland—often in close collaboration and friendship with ships of the Royal Navy similarly engaged. There had, for example, been trouble in Mexico that very summer, and to protect European interests the German light cruiser S.M.S. *Dresden* acted in concert with ships of the British 4th Cruiser Squadron under Rear-Admiral Cradock—a collaboration which received a glowing tribute from the German Envoy in

Mexico in his letter of appreciation to the British Admiral. As it happened, S.M.S. *Dresden* was due for relief at the end of July by another light cruiser, S.M.S. *Karlsruhe*, and so when war was eventually declared on 4 August, and friends of yesterday became bitter antagonists of tomorrow, there were two enemy warships at large somewhere in the Western Atlantic, presumably about to wreak havoc among the Allied or neutral shipping. During the ensuing weeks, these two ships were to prove most elusive.

But it was on the other side of the Americas that the greatest oversea strength of the Imperial German Navy was concentrated. German possessions in the Pacific were many and far-flung. They included the Marianas, the Carolines, the Marshall Islands, Bougainville in the Solomons, German New Guinea and the islands now known as New Ireland and New Britain which lie off that coast, and Samoa. Perhaps most important of all, there was the young and vigorous German colony in the Kiao-chow territory up in the Yellow Sea, grouped about its capital, the naval base of Tsingtao. From this base operated the ships of the German East Asiatic Squadron.

The composition of this squadron was well-known, and so was its reputation. In Whitehall it was recognized as a naval unit of compact strength, excellent morale and high efficiency, officered and led by sailors of character and experience. The information about it which Whitehall lacked, however, was in some ways the most important—the location of its principal ships and the intentions of the officer who commanded them all—and these vital facts were to remain largely matters of constant and rather harassed speculation in the minds of a number of important people, for the best part of three months.

One of the light cruisers of the squadron—*Emden*—did in fact reveal her position much earlier than did the others, for she suddenly appeared in the Bay of Bengal upon a commerce-raiding cruise which paralysed trade in the area, thoroughly frightened business interests from Singapore to Ceylon, and compelled the admiration of all whose pockets, lives or sentiments were not immediately threatened by her activities.

But it was quickly evident that she was operating alone. The other ships of the squadron—*Scharnhorst, Gneisenau, Nürnberg* and *Leipzig*—vanished into the limitless expanse of the Pacific, and although at intervals news would arrive of their sudden appearance at such places as Fanning and Christmas Islands, at Samoa and later off the French port of Papeete at Tahiti, they vanished again long before British or Allied naval forces in the area could concentrate and bring them to action.

Then in the middle of October they arrived at Easter Island, and when the reports reached Whitehall the conclusion hardened that they were heading for South America and the co-operation of the German interests in Chile. This could hardly have come as much of a surprise to the Admiralty, for the alternative courses of action which faced the Commander-in-Chief of the East Asiatic Squadron, once Japan had entered the war on the Allied side, were not very attractive. Whether it was a surprise or not, the fact remained that by the beginning of November an enemy force of considerable strength would be off the west coast of South America, and might shortly afterwards come around the Horn to the east coast. The damage it could then cause among the trade lanes bearing vital supplies of foodstuffs and war materials from the Plate might be so serious as to be fatal, for it was realized that England could be brought to the point of starvation and collapse in six weeks if her oversea trade was brought to a standstill either by action or threat of action. Not all the might of the Grand Fleet would be able to save her in these circumstances.

At all costs the ships of the German East Asiatic Squadron must be found and annihilated before they could bring about such a perilous situation.

But how—and by whom? For British forces in the neighbourhood were woefully inadequate.

CHAPTER ONE

As the harsh afternoon glare softened into twilight on Saturday, 31 October 1914, the slim, low-built shape of a British light cruiser slipped into Coronel Bay and anchored. Her sides were streaked with salt and rust; her boats, though seaworthy, showed signs of rough handling, and the bareness of her upperworks was not entirely due to war conditions. H.M.S. *Glasgow* had come around the Horn from the Falklands in weather which lived well up to its reputation, and had since been battling up and down the Chilean coast in gales which tossed her about like a piece of cork and swept away all fittings not voluntarily removed three months before. She had been hard worked since summer, and now she was battered—but her engines were still sound and her crew alert.

A boat sped away from her side and from the bridge Captain John Luce watched her go, reckoned the odds against them all once again and hoped that Lieutenant Hirst, the Fleet Intelligence Officer, who sat in the boat's sternsheets, would quickly execute the esoteric tricks of his trade, send and collect his telegrams and return on board in short order. Down in the wireless room, as Captain Luce well knew, his telegraphists were listening to the almost continuous, high-singing Telefunken signal-notes which indicated the presence in the immediate vicinity of enemy ships, one call-sign in particular so dominant that he almost expected to see its user, S.M.S. *Leipzig*, sliding into the bay alongside him.

And if the situation to seaward was ominous, it was not improved by conditions ashore. The strong German and pro-German element along the Chilean coast had already proved actively hostile and there was little doubt that someone in Coronel was at that very moment disseminating, through not particularly overt channels, the news that *Glasgow* was in the bay. Thus if the efforts of the Commander-in-Chief of the German East Asiatic Squadron —which must be somewhere close by now—were directed towards cutting off *Glasgow* from the other ships of her squadron, then his task was being greatly facilitated.

Altogether, *Glasgow* was in a tricky situation and Captain Luce was not the only one on board to appreciate it. In the wardroom there was speculation on the chances of getting to sea before the trap was sprung and—less immediately—cool consideration of the chances of battle and subsequent survival, even if they did manage to regain the Flag and thus join company with the armoured cruisers *Monmouth* and *Good Hope* and the armed merchant cruiser *Otranto*, which together formed the command of that ardent, combative little man, Rear-Admiral Sir Christopher Cradock.

Given half a chance, Cradock would fight—that was the general opinion, and despite the almost overwhelming power and efficiency of the enemy squadron, no one doubted that Cradock's course would be the correct one. The last great action in which the Royal Navy had been closely engaged with a powerful antagonist ready for battle was Trafalgar—and for any ship of the British Navy other than a lone scouting cruiser to turn and run from the enemy was unthinkable. Beyond the memory of Nelson gleamed that of Sir Richard Grenville.

About the ship *Glasgow*'s men worked steadily, making good gale damage, cleaning and re-oiling the guns, checking ammunition and trimming the coal bunkers, while all the time the Telefunken signals whined in the ears of the wireless telegraphists. Ashore Lieutenant Hirst talked long and urgently to official and unofficial members of the British service, and it was daylight before he completed his business and returned to *Glasgow*, still with hours of work immediately ahead of him amid the code-books and cyphers of his calling. As he reached his cabin the anchor cable was already coming in, the little cruiser swinging free.

As they cleared the bay there was as yet no immediate sign of the enemy—not that the men aboard *Glasgow* need be unduly worried if it was to be a meeting with the *Leipzig* only, for, on paper at least, there was an exciting equality of strength between them.

Glasgow and *Leipzig* were light cruisers manned by long-service officers and men; they had been in commission for over two years and were thus presumably efficient in seamanship and gunnery, and both were armed with ten 4-inch guns. The German guns were in fact 4.1-inch, and some on board *Glasgow* were aware of the fact that these guns compared very favourably with the older British 6-inch guns. However, to offset this, *Glasgow* herself mounted two more modern 6-inch guns which were reputed to have the range of the old 9-inch batteries.

Should *Glasgow* and *Leipzig* meet then, there appeared the possibility of a single-ship action ensuing, recalling the days of *Shannon* and *Chesapeake*—but reflection revealed the possibility as slight. The old sailing-ships had been independent commands virtually seeking each other out for battle, whereas unless *Leipzig* actually forced an action, the *Glasgow* must first attend to other work and responsibilities, for her primary duty was to return to the Flag and deliver the telegrams and information. Quite possibly, in company with the armoured cruisers and the *Otranto*, a search might then be made for the *Leipzig* which, if successful, would undoubtedly be of fundamental importance, for every chance must be taken to reduce the strength of Admiral von Spee's command before the British and German squadrons met.

Glasgow and *Leipzig* might be reckoned as equals, but the combined British ships in the locality were certainly no match for the crack squadron of the Imperial German Navy. The two German armoured cruisers *Scharnhorst* and *Gneisenau* by themselves would constitute an enormous menace to the heterogeneous collection of ships which composed the British squadron, for the German ships held superiority in speed and also in broadside weight and range.

Add to them the light cruiser *Leipzig* and her two sister ships *Nürnberg* and *Dresden*, and the squadron under Admiral Graf von Spee's command was seen to be an admirably balanced—and modern—fighting force.

Against this force, the British had two elderly armoured cruisers (one of which, according to Hirst, had already been condemned as unfit for further service), one fairly modern light cruiser, and a converted merchantman.

One hope—and one hope only—seemed to exist for even an avoidance of overwhelming defeat, should the ships of the Royal Navy meet the East Asiatic Squadron in force. Somewhere to the south was the old battleship *Canopus*—her exact position was by no means certain—and perhaps with the help of her 12-inch guns the German cruisers could be fought off. But even this was a slim chance, for the guns aboard *Canopus* were as old as herself, and although she had now been for some weeks under Admiral Cradock's command, she had only appeared within his sight twice during that period—on both occasions far off in the distance, labouring up to the rendezvous days late, when circumstances dictated that the Flag could no longer wait for her. Her engines were in such a state of disrepair that the voyage down from the Mediterranean to the Falkland Islands had practically crippled them, and the hasty overhaul carried out at Port Stanley had been barely sufficient to get her round the Horn.

But if Cradock couldn't wait for the *Canopus*, perhaps the battle would—should Fate prove kind. It was at least arguable that von Spee would keep his distance if her four 12-inch guns were present in the British battle-line, although whether it was right for ships of a navy which held the example of Horatio Nelson in its highest tradition, even to *wish* for the enemy to keep his distance—let alone to rely upon his doing so—was open to question.

However, if *Glasgow*, *Monmouth* and *Good Hope* could catch isolated units of von Spee's command and thus deal with it piece-meal, then the whole strategic situation in the Southern Seas might be successfully dealt with.

But it seemed rather a lot to hope for.

At sea again, *Glasgow* steered first north (whilst still within sight of curious eyes) and then Captain Luce took his ship around to the south-west, plunging ahead into wind and a rising sea as fast as the engines would take her, in order to deliver the telegrams and naval intelligence into Cradock's hands without breaking wireless silence. Seas swept the foredeck, spume drowned the bridge and the wind sang in the signal halliards.

Four hours later *Glasgow* rejoined the Flag some forty miles west of Coronel Bay. *Good Hope* and *Monmouth* were there, rolling like barrels, and the *Otranto* developed a list whenever she came broadside to the wind. There was no sign of the *Canopus*.

The seas were far too heavy for boatwork, so *Glasgow* towed a cask containing the vital papers across *Good Hope*'s bows—and in the ruling weather conditions she was both extremely lucky and extremely adept, for the manœuvre was immediately successful. It was also to some effect, for by two o'clock a string of signals were fluttering from the *Good Hope*'s halliards, and Captain Luce's appreciation of the situation was confirmed.

The squadron were to form line abreast, about fifteen miles apart with *Good Hope* to the west and *Glasgow* to the east of the line, and sweep north-west by north at ten knots. The signals preceded by *Leipzig*'s call-sign still bleated loud through the dull-grey afternoon, and Kit Cradock had decided that she was to be found and annihilated before the heavy might of the German armoured cruisers could come to her protection. For this task the guns of the *Canopus* would not be necessary.

Outwards through the lumpy waves the squadron spread—cold, wet, and pitching now on the steep following sea : *Good Hope*, with the valiant little Admiral aboard treasuring the honour and reputation of the Royal Navy above all else; *Monmouth*, with her crew of Scottish fishermen and coastguards, her twelve young naval cadets fresh from Dartmouth, and her outdated engines kept going only by superhuman efforts on the part of Engineer-Commander Wilshin and his staff; *Otranto* loomed like a haystack out of the tumbled seas; *Glasgow* plunged on, grim and hard-bitten. Officers and men with enough experience to cause them misgivings kept them to themselves.

It was part of the pattern of that day that *Glasgow* should see the smoke first. She reported it to the Flag and moved off to starboard to investigate, with *Otranto* still in company (for the sweep line had not yet formed) and *Monmouth* only four miles astern. The cloud grew wider as it came up over the horizon, and as *Glasgow* approached, it was seen to have three stems. By 4.25 p.m. *Scharnhorst* and *Gneisenau* were recognizable, and astern of the armoured cruisers came the *Leipzig* whose signals had baited the trap. *Glasgow* steamed nearer to establish the course, while incredibly, the enemy squadron remained apparently unaware of her presence.

Then at 4.30 p.m. black smoke belched from the German funnels as von Spee ordered full steam for a chase, and *Glasgow* turned to race back towards the Flag. Immediately she turned, her telegraphists were deafened by the scream in their earphones as German keyboards jammed her signals—but by 4.45 p.m. Cradock knew that the meeting he had long anticipated was at hand, and he also knew the strength of the enemy force in sight and their course. He ordered concentration on *Glasgow* and formation of the battle-line, and at 5.10 p.m. on that grey, squall-swept Sunday afternoon, the British ships were together and turning.

At this moment the armoured strength of the opposing force was nearly fifteen miles away, and the German squadron had yet more units detached. For the British ships—even against such preponderant strength—it might still be possible to attain some success if conditions of wind and sea could be used to advantage, and with this in mind the British line was formed by 5.30 p.m. and was driving south-east across the rising sea—*Good Hope* leading, then *Monmouth*, *Glasgow* and the huge, lumbering, thin-skinned *Otranto*—in an effort to secure the inshore position. Once there the wind would blow the British smoke clear of the guns while at the same time it blanketed the *Scharnhorst*'s black pall across the German gun-sights.

There was even a chance that if the British could win through to

6

this position, they might whilst doing so, execute the classic naval manœuvre of crossing the enemy's T, and at the moment of passing thus bring their whole broadside weight to bear upon *Scharnhorst* at a time when she could only reply with her foredeck guns and be masking those of her consort. But by 5.45 p.m. the hopes were falling. The gap between the squadrons had narrowed —and von Spee's ships were working up to twenty knots whilst *Otranto* was holding the British back to fifteen. She was almost as much of a drag as *Canopus* would have been, without however the possible compensation of 12-inch guns.

By 5.50 p.m. it was evident that the race was lost.

At six o'clock Admiral Cradock ordered a turn away to the south—they were then four points to starboard of an enemy who obviously had both the intention and speed to keep them there : for the Germans a battle in line, broadside pounding against broadside, held every advantage.

But there were still some benefits to be obtained from factors of light and wind. The clouds were broken and the sun was sinking. If the British could close the range with the setting sun behind them, it would serve to blind the German gun-layers whilst at the same time light up the German ships into perfect targets. Somehow Cradock must close until *Monmouth*'s old 6-inch guns—and perhaps even *Glasgow*'s puny 4-inch armament—could inflict damage, for at long range there were only *Good Hope*'s two 9.2-inch guns to battle it out with twelve 8.2-inch guns which *Scharnhorst* and *Gneisenau* could bring to bear—although possibly *Glasgow*'s modern 6-inch guns might be able to play some part.

At 6.04 p.m. then, the Admiral ordered each of his ships to turn four points towards the enemy, and in line abreast they steamed towards them, rolling their casemates awash in the broadside seas.

Von Spee turned his squadron away and kept his distance. He would not come to action yet.

Thwarted, and to ease the labours of his battling squadron, Cradock turned back to a southerly course, re-formed his battle-line and grimly watched the strength arraying itself against him. *Leipzig* had closed up and *Dresden* was now racing in over the horizon only a mile astern of her; doubtless *Nürnberg* would soon arrive.

Eighteen thousand yards separated the two lines.

To the west the British line still rolled until their main-deck guns were awash and spray drenched telescopes and gun-sights, encrusting them with salt—*Good Hope, Monmouth, Glasgow, Otranto*—for what use a merchantman would be in a naval battle.

To the east steamed the Germans, their guns high above the waterline, their equipment better than their enemy's—and dry. *Scharnhorst, Gneisenau, Leipzig, Dresden.*

The scene was set, but hardly for a battle. Only a miracle could avert a massacre. Two old armoured cruisers, one light cruiser and one armed merchantman, were pitted against two modern armoured cruisers with two, and perhaps three, light cruisers. Two British 9.2-inch guns and two 6-inch guns to answer at long range twelve 8.2-inch guns. Even at short range the odds were not appreciably less, for the Germans fired a broadside of 3,812 pounds against the British 2,815.

Most significant of all—and most tragic—against some two thousand two hundred fully-trained, long-service German sailors who were reckoned among the most efficient in the Imperial German Navy, were to fight a similar number of Britons, the vast majority of whom had been happily pursuing civilian vocations less than six months before, and who now had little more than their pride and their courage to give them confidence.

But they had their Admiral—and whether he was brave or quixotic, resolute or reckless, impelled by the simplicity of high honour or by incredible stupidity—it seems that Kit Cradock had their hearts. When at 6.18 p.m. he wirelessed to *Canopus*, still trudging up through the seas over two hundred and fifty miles away to the south, 'I am going to attack the enemy now!' they cheered him as their forefathers had cheered a hundred and nine years before, drifting down on to the Franco-Spanish crescent.

From *Good Hope*'s masthead fluttered the battle-ensign, and from her halliards the signal, 'Follow in the Admiral's wake'.

Carefully, imperceptibly, the British line edged in towards the enemy, striving for a converging course, hoping to close the range.

Five minutes later, *Scharnhorst* led the German line away one point to the eastward and the lines were parallel again. From the British decks men watched across the grey waste in silence and grim resolve.

The scene was now one of ominous clarity. *Scharnhorst* and *Gneisenau* rode powerfully over the seas, the details of their high-placed heavy armament picked out by the westering sun, the seas racing along the towering sides and occasionally sweeping the fore-decks. Behind the armoured ships came the light cruisers, crashing through the seas with only the upper-deck guns workable : it was some slight consolation to the British to know that at least the weaker units of the enemy force suffered the same discomforts as themselves.

For another half-hour the two battle-lines plunged southwards in parallel lines at about sixteen knots—the highest speed of which *Otranto* was capable. Then behind the British, the sun's rim touched the horizon and as it slid down to become first a semi-circle and then a gradually-diminishing segment, the conditions of light began to change.

Evening crept over the sea from the east and touched the German battle-line, greying it into the sea and the sky beyond. As twilight thickened, the moon came up behind heavy clouds to show fleetingly through them, briefly outlining the enemy ships— and now it seemed that *Scharnhorst* and *Gneisenau* were closing in. Von Spee was edging forward. To the west, the afterglow of the sun made a fiery, yellow-shot tapestry of the windswept sky against which the British ships stood out in black, hard-edged relief. Nothing would help them tonight but their courage and their pride in the long tradition of the Royal Navy.

At 7.04 p.m. on Sunday, 1 November 1914, the 8.2-inch guns of the German East Asiatic Squadron at last opened fire upon the British ships, at a range of 12,000 yards.

From the bridge of *Glasgow* were seen two lines of orange flashes

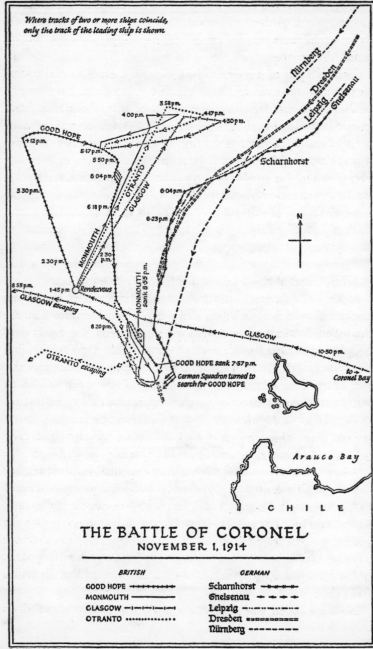

THE BATTLE OF CORONEL
NOVEMBER 1, 1914

from *Scharnhorst* and *Gneisenau*, and as the thunder of *Good Hope*'s
9.2s answered, grey-white mushrooms blossomed from the sea
five hundred yards short of the British flagship, beautifully aimed,
beautifully grouped.

Glasgow's pair of modern 6-inch guns fired experimentally into
the darkness, but even while the gunnery-control officer was vainly
searching the east for some sign of fall of shot, the orange lines
sparkled again and then again—and the lines were lengthened now
as *Leipzig* and *Dresden* opened fire. For a few more brief seconds,
only the crash of the seas and the sounds of their own movements
were heard by *Glasgow*'s crew—then shell splinters whined shrilly
overhead, the seas erupted around them, *Monmouth* ahead steamed
through a forest of water and *Good Hope*'s foredeck exploded in a
sheet of flame, which twisted the fore 9.2-inch gun into a hopeless,
useless knot of steel protruding from a turret like a blazing
cauldron.

Before the mind could react, the next salvo arrived.

Monmouth's foredeck flared up in hard-edged flame and black
smoke billowed from sudden, sharp fires along her port side. As
she rolled, her gun-crews fought their guns—still hopelessly out-
ranged by the German guns which now straddled the British line
along its length, filling the night with screaming shells and the
vicious irritating whine of splinters. *Good Hope*'s deck amidships
threw up a fan of sparks, her upper bridge, masthead and foretop
glowed redly as high-explosive shell from the *Scharnhorst* burst
against them, then the glow died as cordite flared on the deck
below, and ammunition exploded whitely along the gun-deck.

Alongside the looming *Otranto*, water spouted up to reach her
deck level. She drew out of line on to *Glasgow*'s port quarter and
as her huge bulk made an excellent ranging device for the enemy,
her captain took her away to the westward—though not before she
had been neatly triangulated by three shells from *Gneisenau*, whose
gunnery was upholding her claim to the Kaiser's Gold Cup. One
of the minor miracles of the day was *Otranto*'s unscathed departure
from the line.

Now the action was at its thickest. With the early loss of *Good*

Hope's fore 9.2, the British chances of harming the enemy at anything but short range had been halved—and with no alternative, Cradock led across the shell-torn seas to bring the 6-inch guns of the flagship and *Monmouth* into action. The after 9.2-inch still fired—once a minute!—but its noise and flame was lost amid the holocaust which raged around it, for ammunition blazed fiercely and fire was already spreading through the flagship's decks below.

Still they plunged across towards the German line, still the shells crashed into them and still flame scoured the decks. Then both *Good Hope* and *Monmouth* turned broadside to their antagonists and the port 6-inch batteries burst into action. Hope and feverish activity galvanized the gun-crews; salvo after salvo thundered from the gun-decks.

Abruptly, *Gneisenau*'s guns shortened range, one of her high-explosive shells hit *Monmouth*'s fore-turret, blew off the roof and burnt out the housing. As flames licked up out of the steel shell, a violent explosion shattered the forecastle and when its anger died, no sign of gun or turret remained.

Then ominously, *Monmouth*'s ports glowed redly in the gathering darkness as burning cordite turned the narrow confines of her mess decks into choking hells. Still *Gneisenau*'s shells crashed through her decks and exploded with sickening violence amid the shambles below. An armour-piercing shell came through the side abreast of the after funnel, passed through the body of the ship and exploded among ammunition stacked for the starboard battery. A curtain of flame spread upwards along the starboard side, outlining the upperworks in black against dull red streaked with green, and twisting, tortured debris cartwheeled away into the night.

As though beaten out of line by sheer weight of metal, *Monmouth* began to sag away to starboard, losing speed as she did so until *Glasgow*, still punching up through the seas astern of her, had to drop away in order to avoid masking her still-defiant though now sporadic fire—in order too, to avoid entering the zone of fire still laid down by the indefatigable German gunners. Again the shells found *Monmouth*. Flames burst out on her quarterdeck, she listed heavily to port, her head was lower and her fire slackened. Heavy seas flooded through gaping bows and dragged her away from the line—but she was not yet beaten, and to those on board *Glasgow* who could spare her a glance it looked at this time as though she was having some success in overcoming the fires within, which now sulked dully in the darkness.

But she never rejoined the line, and as time passed her guns lapsed into silence.

Except for the endless flashes from their batteries, the enemy were by now quite invisible.

Not so *Good Hope*. She flared like a beacon.

Since action had commenced the British flagship had received the undivided attention of the gunners aboard *Scharnhorst*, who had first hit her with their third salvo, and who since then had been firing at her—coolly and extremely competently—at a rate of nearly four salvoes every minute.

By 7.23 p.m., the range was down to 6,600 yards.

On through the raging and shell-torn sea, Kit Cradock held the converging course—so steadily in fact, that von Spee began to suspect a torpedo attack and edged off another point to eastward. Still the shells crashed into *Good Hope*, ripping away her decks and bulkheads, bursting in the crowded flats, spreading fire and chaos through her riven hull: still, stubbornly, she pushed on through the waves, her port 6-inch battery defiant, but firing slowly and spasmodically now as gun-crews perished in the consuming flames or were cut down by flying steel. At 7.40 p.m., she seemed to slow and stagger under the rain of blows. Yet another fire blazed up on her foredeck, and the clouds of steam and smoke which billowed around her glowed sullenly in its light —but she still was moving towards the enemy.

A sheet of flame played continuously along her sides upon which the seas had no effect. She might roll until her casemates were awash but as she heaved herself up again, the flames flickered weirdly, almost caressingly, between the waterline and the deck-rails, almost as though they were persuading her, pleading with her, to cease her efforts and give herself up to their gentle cremation.

As if in contemptuous reply, at 7.42 p.m., *Good Hope* gathered up all her remaining strength, turned directly towards her tormentors and charged them. Firing as she went, she heaved her stricken weight over the mounting seas trailing flame and wreathing clouds behind her—and as von Spee ordered his ships out of her course, there was for a few brief moments a pause to her agony. Then abruptly both *Scharnhorst* and *Gneisenau* opened fire upon her with full broadsides; blanketed under a dreadful fire, she was at last brought to a halt with her upper deck a sea of flame, and her last desperate throw defeated.

As though stunned, she drifted down silently between the lines.

Then the fires reached a main magazine and at 7.53 p.m.—fifty minutes after the first salvo had been fired at her—*Good Hope* was shattered by an explosion which still lives in the memories of those who witnessed it. A broad column of flame rose upwards from between her main and aftermost funnel until it towered two hundred feet above her decks, and in its awful light jagged and incongruous shapes soared up and away into the darkness, twisting and weaving in the blast, tumbling in the sudden vacuums.

The thunder of the explosion dwarfed the racket of the guns and echoed leagues across the sea to the Chilean coast. On the *Nürnberg*—still six miles to the north—men held their hands to their ears, while nearer, in the ships still engaged, the clangour swelled out of the realm of noise and became a physical force battering through the defences of the skull to get at the naked tissues of the brain itself.

Then the column of fire broke, flooding outwards at its base to wash along the decks and fill the gutted hull with lazy waves of fire. Debris crashed down into the sea, the whole mass of the forepart of the ship silently detached itself and slid down into oblivion, and incredibly, two 6-inch guns of the port battery aft each fired twice into the darkness.

Then the waves took the blazing cradle of pain and defiance further off into the darkness, the flames sulked, the pall above glowed luridly, and all that remained of Kit Cradock and his men drifted out of the battle.

And, for the moment, the battle was done.

Glasgow had borne a charmed life.

Circumstance had also added a most bizarre note to the atmosphere in which she played her part in the battle, for at the outbreak of war her commission on the South American station had been almost complete and many of her complement had acquired parrots to take home to England. When action became inevitable, these birds—some sixty of them—were released from their cages and given a chance to escape to the mainland. They rose in a cloud of brilliant blues and greens and oranges, then possibly because of a group unwillingness to risk the rising power of the gale they all settled back on *Glasgow*'s upperworks and remained there despite all attempts to scare them away.

When the first salvoes thundered out, they rose again, cawing and screaming madly, but as the battle wore on they gradually ceased their protests and returned to the ship, clinging drunkenly to stays and yards until either violent movement or their own failing strength loosened their hold. Then they would lurch down towards the deck or bridge and become engulfed in the activity of war, generally either to be swept overboard or knocked aside by hurrying feet. Two of them perched side by side on one of the 6-inch gun barrels, where they remained until rendered unconscious by the repeated crash and fury beneath them. As the action progressed so the numbers fell, and only ten were eventually recovered.

Incredibly, this loss of the parrots was almost the heaviest casualty sustained by the cruiser. It was afterward estimated that some six hundred shells were fired at *Glasgow*, but some protecting fate guarded her from all except five, of which three lodged harmlessly in her coal bunkers, one entered and broke up against a conning-tower support without exploding (though it wrecked the captain's pantry), another burst aft, just above the port outer propeller, and tore an irregular hole in the ship's side just as though she had been rammed. It flooded one compartment but did nothing to affect *Glasgow*'s steaming abilities.

In return, *Glasgow* had engaged both *Leipzig* and *Dresden* for the major part of the batttle and at the end, in fury and desperation, she had taken on *Gneisenau* and *Scharnhorst*, and even hit the latter ship with one of her puny 4-inch shells, which however, apparently exhausted itself on the journey and failed to explode on arrival. But with *Good Hope* and *Monmouth* out of the fight, every time *Glasgow* fired, the whole enemy line answered and she steamed through chaos.

At 8.03 p.m. with *Good Hope* gone and the enemy invisible, Captain Luce ordered cease fire, and then took his ship around to the west to find, and offer succour to, *Monmouth*. When he found her, the badly battered cruiser was listing and her head was still down, but her upper decks were no longer aflame and only the port-holes below the quarterdeck still glowed.

But the tragedy was not yet ended.

As *Glasgow* bore up to render what assistance she could, the moon made one of its rare appearances to light up a tumultuous sea, a torn ship—and four enemy ships sweeping in search for them. If *Monmouth* could turn her stern to sea she might last, and if she could hold the north-west course she might, by the grace of God, keep clear of the German line—and perhaps even limp as far as the Chilean coast; but *Glasgow* must leave her or perish.

She signalled to *Monmouth* twice, passed close under her stern, and with wretched misery aboard at the thought of the compulsory desertion, steamed west and away into the darkness. *Glasgow*, alone among the British squadron, had speed, and soon it was evident that she must have shaken off any pursuit and was free to turn south to race after *Otranto* for the Magellan Straits, her wireless at last clear of the enemy attempts to jam it and able to tell the dreadful story to *Canopus*, still labouring up miles to the south.

For a time, there was hope that *Monmouth* had eluded the enemy and was limping towards some sort of safety. But at nine o'clock firing broke out again to the north, and with ice in their hearts the men aboard *Glasgow* counted the gun-flashes and watched a searchlight poke its pallid fingers over the horizon. *Nürnberg* had found her.

Captain von Schönberg had known from the moment he received the first signal ordering formation of the battle-line, that his chances of getting *Nürnberg* into position were extremely remote. Her boilers were in sad need of repair, her engines of replacement and her port propeller of two new blades—so despite the eagerness with which he and his officers might stare into the torn, growling darkness ahead, he knew that their hopes of adding to the tumult were small. The wind from the south howled through the stays, the seas swept the forecastle and flooded the conning-tower—and *Nürnberg* piledrove through them in an effort to reach the battle.

Then came the explosion—and apparently the end—and although much relief was felt when wireless signals indicated the highly satisfactory result, there was some disappointment and dissatisfaction at the role of spectator which *Nürnberg* had played.

Then at 8.35 p.m. the look-out reported a column of smoke on the starboard bow, for which von Schönberg at once steered. Apparently the smoke must have been made by *Glasgow*, for although no mention is made of *Nürnberg* in Captain Luce's report, von Schönberg chased the British ship until she disappeared from sight, her speed taking her rapidly over the horizon.

As *Nürnberg* turned back towards the ships of her squadron, von Schönberg saw *Monmouth* against the light of the moon. The armoured cruiser was listing, but she was undoubtedly under way.

At first von Schönberg thought that he had come across one of the ships of his own squadron, so he bore down on her from the south-west, making the agreed recognition signal and passing close to port. There was no reply, but not wishing to harm a friend, he closed in and switched on his searchlight. It picked out first the white ensign—still flying—then the details of the torn and shattered hull, then the working-parties scurrying about the decks. Foam threshed under her stern. *Monmouth* was making progress.

In fairness to von Schönberg it must be stated that he gave *Monmouth* every chance to haul down her flag. He waited some minutes before opening fire, his searchlight still pointedly illuminating the white ensign from some six hundred yards away. His first salvoes were from 4-inch guns aimed high, and although when this brought about no lowering of the flag, he fired a torpedo at *Monmouth*, he was not upset when it failed to explode in *Monmouth*'s hull, having possibly passed underneath the rolling ship.

He then ceased fire and waited for *Monmouth*'s next move.

It was not long in coming. She seemed to gather speed and begin to turn—and two of von Schönberg's officers on deck heard instructions shouted from *Monmouth*'s bridge ordering the men back to the guns from their tasks about the ship. Either the intention was to ram *Nürnberg*, or turn to bring the starboard guns to bear upon her.

There is no need to doubt the regret with which von Schönberg states he then acted, but unless *Monmouth* hauled down her flag, his course—his duty—was obvious. As *Monmouth* circled, so did *Nürnberg*—at twice the speed—and as the German light cruiser came round close under *Monmouth*'s stern, she opened fire on the unprotected part of her hull, tearing it open and ripping the decks apart. Under the onslaught, *Monmouth* shuddered and listed over further and further. The seas washed up to the port deck-rail, then across to flood around the funnels.

Slowly, still under a hail of shell, *Monmouth* leaned completely over and capsized. At 8.58 p.m. the waters closed above her stern —from which her flag had flown until the end.

Nürnberg was hardly to be envied for her unhappy part—and indeed letters and reports written by her officers do not make happy or triumphant reading. She did her duty.

So did *Monmouth*.

But on *Glasgow*, as she punched her way southwards through the head sea, bitterness kindled a slow fire of anger within those who had fought and toiled aboard her. The men of *Monmouth* had cheered *Glasgow* as she left them to their fate and within the darker skein of men's voices, a boy's treble had woven a golden thread.

Now the voice was silenced.

CHAPTER TWO

To the men aboard *Canopus* far away to the south, it had been a night of frustration and distress. When at nine o'clock Captain Heathcote Grant read the signal from *Glasgow* revealing that the squadron had been scattered, he realized that although he now had no hope of taking his ship into the main battle-line, there might still be work for him to do. *Glasgow* at least was still afloat and coming south at twenty-four knots; calculation showed that the two ships must be about two hundred miles apart and as there was always a possibility that accident or ill-luck might still cause the light cruiser to fall prey to the enemy squadron, Captain Grant held course through the darkness. He was making, he considered, fifteen knots, so in five hours *Glasgow* and *Canopus* should be level and on parallel but opposite courses. They might even meet.

At 2 a.m., however, no sound or sign of battle had penetrated the wrack of the night and he concluded that *Glasgow* must be safe but over the seaward horizon. He therefore turned his lumbering command through sixteen points and headed south, his speed immediately dropping to nine knots as he exchanged the aid of the southerly gale for its opposition. As night wore on, the wind abated and the seas became less angry so *Canopus* managed to work up to ten and a half knots, and when daylight came she was plunging on down through a grey, empty sea, abreast but out of sight of the Chonos Archipelago.

It was time to take stock.

Glasgow by now must be well past and away to the south and west. *Otranto*, according to *Glasgow*'s signal, was even further out in the Pacific, probably making down for the Horn as her bulk precluded dainty manœuvring through the winding, treacherous channels which led into the Magellan Straits—and in any case if she was the object of a search she could hide more easily in the wide oceans.

The enemy were to northward—their movements problematical.

If they were coming south—and it seemed best to act upon the assumption that they were—then it could only be a matter of hours before they overtook *Canopus*, and although from a purely personal point of view Captain Grant would not have objected to a chance of turning his 12-inch guns on the *Scharnhorst*, there were other considerations to bear in mind. For instance, after the pounding which the engines of his ship had taken during the previous evening in his attempt to get her up into the battle-area, it was quite likely that they would shortly break down again, and he did not think much of his chances of successfully avenging his Admiral, if he were forced to attempt to do so from a drifting hulk. Neither did he feel that in the event of fundamental repairs becoming necessary, the open sea was the best place for his engineers to undertake them.

During the forenoon of the day following the battle, therefore, he altered course one point towards the coast, kept the Taitao Peninsula to port and entered the Gulf of Penas that evening. He was now in sheltered waters and as his engines had as yet evinced no more signs of trouble than was usual, he decided to risk taking *Canopus* straight on down towards Magellan.

The following morning he edged his battleship down into the tortuous—and for a ship of that size virtually uncharted—Messier Channel, between Wellington Island and the Chilean coast. Glaciers dropped to the water's edge on either hand, wide and deeply-indented fjords tempted him off the main channel, the cold of ever-shadowed waters arose and penetrated the bones of all on board, and mist threatened to turn to gelid fog and bring to a complete halt the already painful progress.

Yet *Canopus* must hurry, for if von Spee were coming south, he must not be allowed to reach and occupy the Magellan Straits before *Canopus* arrived at the western entrance. Somehow, the battleship must reach the Straits, join forces with *Glasgow*, and with her make for the Falkland Islands to prepare some form of defence for Port Stanley and the naval installations there.

On southwards through the Messier Channel *Canopus* groped her way, emerging at last through the southern exit between Madre de Dios and Hanover Islands, then back into the channels of the Queen Adelaide Archipelago, through the Smythe Channel and late on 4 November—three days after the battle—out into Magellan.

There was for the moment no sign of the German ships, and *Canopus* hurried on through the Straits after *Glasgow*, who, Captain Grant learned, was well ahead of them and already through the Gonzalez Channel and heading up for Punta Arenas. There was news of *Otranto* too—she was safe and closing Ildefonso Island on the southern tip of South America, heading for the Horn passage. Now the three British ships were coming together again, crawling along a coastline as stark and bleak as any in five continents, with a nomenclature which reads like a catalogue of doom : Desolation Island, Fatal Bay, Dislocation Harbour, Useless Bay, Deceit Island, Fury Harbour, Last Hope Inlet, Port Famine.

Set in ice, the scenery accorded with their mood.

It took two more days for *Canopus* to pass through the Straits, and at the eastern end under the Cape of the Eleven Thousand Virgins, she found *Glasgow* awaiting her. *Otranto* was at the Horn and with ample coal aboard she was instructed to take herself away out of danger up to Montevideo, but both coaling and strategic considerations indicated another destination for *Glasgow* and *Canopus*. Three hundred miles to the east lay the Falkland Islands, their base and an undisputed British possession for the last eighty years. From it the ships of Admiral Cradock's squadron had sailed for the Chilean coast, and it could be assumed that to it Admiral von Spee would shortly direct his attentions.

Glasgow and *Canopus* sailed at once and by the morning of

8 November were at anchor and coaling in Port Stanley. The outlook was not bright.

The Falkland Islands at this time had a civilian population of over a thousand crofters and fishermen—mostly of Scottish descent or origin—who farmed sheep on its moors or trawled its coasts, both so similar to those of the Outer Hebrides from which so many of them came. There was a wireless station there, a landlocked harbour with an outer bay in which battleships could moor, and dockyard facilities which the Admiralty had installed during the previous decade.

Most important of all, there was coal—enough to fill the bunkers of a cruiser squadron several times over—and if British ships were not to use it then at least it must be prevented from falling into enemy hands. At first sight it seemed best to fire the dumps, and certainly if the islands were to be abandoned—however temporarily —this should be done.

If the islands were to be abandoned.

Neither the warships nor the wireless station were in direct touch with London (wireless, it must be remembered, had still many years of development in front of it, and in any case atmospheric conditions in the area are notorious), and without either definite instructions or at least an indication of the Admiralty's plans, precipitate action might render a bad situation infinitely worse.

Before they could justifiably issue instructions for so irrevocable a stroke as firing the coal dumps, both Captain Luce and Captain Grant felt that they should know more of the overall strategic situation.

What were the Admiralty's intentions?

How was Britain reacting to the Coronel disaster?

CHAPTER THREE

BRITAIN was reacting violently.

When the news of the battle appeared in the newspapers on the evening of 5 November, public feeling seems to have been divided between bewilderment and anger : bewilderment at this demonstration that the Royal Navy was apparently not as invincible as all had been brought up to believe, and anger at this condition. In anger, they looked for someone to blame, and as the arguments as to who was responsible for the defeat at Coronel are not likely ever to be completely settled, it might be as well first of all to examine them, and also the various factors which had brought about the deployment of a weak British squadron against the overwhelming power of the German ships.

Responsibility for the catastrophe at Coronel has been laid at many doors. The Admiralty has been blamed for the ambiguity of its instructions to Admiral Cradock, and Cradock of course has received strong criticism for accepting action against such powerful odds under the conditions of wind and light which prevailed at the time of the action, instead of retiring rapidly with his force until he had reached the protection of the 12-inch guns of *Canopus*. On a broader field, Parliament has also been reproached for not providing the Royal Navy with a larger cruiser fleet—and as an unspoken corollary, presumably the British Public were to blame for not voting for different members, although in view of subsequent events perhaps the choice of these latter two is a little wild.

It does seem at first sight as though some degree of responsibility would lie between the first and second choices.

In the *Official History of Naval Operations of the Great War*, Sir Julian Corbett presents a well-argued case against the Admiralty. In it, he quotes the telegrams which the First Lord of the Admiralty sent to Cradock and the memoranda bearing what have since become the world's most famous initials which passed between the various Admiralty departments, and he then goes on to outline the alternatives of action with which Cradock was presumably faced. It is a little disconcerting to find that Mr Churchill quotes substantially the same telegrams and memoranda in his spirited defence of the Admiralty (see *The World Crisis*, Vol. 1) and uses them to illustrate somewhat different alternatives.

In support of the official historian, there was certainly one Admiralty telegram which might have been less ambiguously worded —but then one of Admiral Cradock's positively invited interpretation in a manner very different from that which his subsequent actions show to have been his intention. Between Whitehall and *Good Hope* there was undoubtedly much misunderstanding, but examination of the writings of the principle characters concerned reveals a basic difference of attitude (though not of character) which went far deeper than mere words.

It is a question as to whether Mr Churchill can be blamed for assuming that he was addressing his instructions to a man as deeply versed in the military strategies of Marlborough and Wellington (who did not accept action unless they possessed superiority in numbers) as he was in the naval tradition of Nelson, who accepted action upon the usually correct assumption that he possessed superiority in spirit, character and efficiency. But nobody at the Admiralty apparently thought it necessary to point out to the First Lord that not everybody possessed his own sense of history or his knowledge of it.

This is not to say that Kit Cradock was uneducated—far from it—but he had joined the Royal Navy when he was thirteen and to all intents and purposes his formal schooling had then ended. His whole life had been dedicated to his own Service, and although he could undoubtedly have rattled off the names of Nelson's 'Band of Brothers' and given detailed and accurate accounts of the actions at Aboukir Bay, Copenhagen and Trafalgar, it is possible that he could not have named Wellington's subordinates or listed off-hand Marlborough's battles. Nelson's attitude and tactics—even at Teneriffe—Cradock understood and applauded, but the reasons for Wellington's retreat behind the Lines of Torres Vedras he had probably never read, let alone studied.

Cradock had occupied some of his leisure hours with writing, and had, in all, three books published. The last one, *Whispers from the Fleet*, is a friendly, avuncular volume intended for the guidance of the young naval officer, and Cradock's knowledge of soldiers and their profession, and his attitude to them, are aptly illustrated in the following passage which occurs at the beginning of the section dealing with transports :

> Varied as are the duties of the Naval Service, I think that this particular job, i.e.,—The conveyance of our brother the soldier—who is always, bless him, in a slow hurry—from one portion of the globe to another, is generally voted by sailors as a tiresome duty : and while he (the soldier) goes out to all the pomp and glory of war, his friend in blue remains behind, and by harder work tries to smother his feelings, and to forget that he too, would like to fight. Nevertheless, the transport work for the Empire must be done, and done by the Navy *alone*; and not only so, but performed with all the willingness, good temper, and self-control gained from our training.

As during Cradock's life, our military—as apart from naval—adventures had included the Boer War, the never-ending strife along the North-West Frontier, the Sudan Campaign and even the closing stages of the dreadful, disease-ridden Crimean War, it is significant that in this context he could write of 'the pomp and glory of war'.

This is not to pour scorn on Cradock or his ideas, but a man who wrote thus, and of 'our brother, the soldier—bless him' is unlikely to have been a keen student of Napoleon's Maxims (which have been often quoted against him) or in the strategies of the Duke who referred to his Peninsular veterans as 'the scum of the earth, enlisted for drink'.

And if he *had* read them, it is evident from both his life and his writings that he profoundly disagreed with at least that portion of them which insists that numerical superiority is essential for success in battle. The last chapter of *Whispers from the Fleet* reads as follows :

> Which faction is it, the 'Blue Water', or the 'Blue Funk School' which is for ever writing to the newspapers to prove, that because one nation will have six and a half battleships built in three years, and another four and a quarter commenced next month : unless we immediately do *something*, we shall in ten years time, be seven-eighths of a battleship behind the combined navies of the world—not forgetting that of Timbuctoo ?

When reading the above it should be remembered that Cradock was a man of his day and so was his style of writing. To men of his day—and not only Englishmen—the majesty and invincibility of the Royal Navy was a cornerstone of life, and of the components of that cornerstone, the intangible were of the higher importance. Courage, honour and the unbroken tradition were paramount : ships and their gun-power were of secondary nature, and David, if his heart were pure, would always defeat Goliath.

There had even been events in Cradock's own Service career to confirm him in this attitude, perhaps the most typical being the occasion in 1900 when he led a mixed force of British, German, Japanese and Italian sailors in the assault on the Boxer-held Taku Forts, on the Peiho River.

In broad daylight and across a sun-baked mudflat without a vestige of cover, Cradock led his assorted force towards the parapet and the West Gate of the Fort beyond. They were under fire from two field guns, and the embrasures of the fort were packed with riflemen whose fire was sufficiently accurate to cause enough casualties for the Italian contingent, and even some of the Germans, to decide upon a course of discretion. But the Bluejackets, the Japanese and the majority of the Germans, ignoring everything but the stentorian voice of their leader—doubling smartly ahead, some seventy yards in front of his leading files—advanced steadily in open formation, deployed upon his command through a gap between the moat and the river, and charged up the slope of the fort, with Cradock and a Japanese sailor racing each other for the honour of being first over the top. Close behind them were two midshipmen—one of whom remarked to the other as they bore down upon the demoralized enemy, that in that last sprint, 'he had put up a couple of snipe!'

It is not really surprising that a man whose life included such an incident should stand and fight, fourteen years later, off the South American coast. He had led Englishmen against an apparently unassailable citadel before—and won. However different the physical factors may have been, all Kit Cradock's instincts must have prompted him to attack von Spee, and his instincts were supported by his training and his beliefs.

And what exactly were his alternatives?

He had not expected to meet the East Asiatic Squadron upon that grey Sunday afternoon. He was pursuing, he believed (as did all the officers of his squadron) one light cruiser—*Leipzig*. In such a pursuit the armed merchantman *Otranto* had a part to play and he was completely justified in keeping her with him. But once *Scharnhorst* and *Gneisenau* appeared, *Otranto* became a dragging liability in need of protection. The merchantman barely managed sixteen knots that afternoon, and had she been left to her fate she would have fallen a helpless prey to *Leipzig* or *Dresden*, without even the consolation that her sacrifice had materially relieved the pressure on the other ships of the squadron.

His critics state that Cradock should have retreated with his cruisers until he gained the addition of the 12-inch guns aboard *Canopus* to his battle-line. 'With *Canopus*,' says Mr Churchill, '. . . Cradock was safe'—but even without the official historian's comment that safety was a conception unknown to the Admiral, there would appear to be flaws in this argument.

The following table giving the ranges of the guns which would have been in action had *Canopus* been present, is given in one of the reports upon the battle :

Canopus	12-in.	Approx.	12,000yds.	6-in.	(QF)	Approx.	9,000yds.
Good Hope	9.2 ,,	,,	12,500 ,,	6 ,,	(BL)	,,	10,000 ,,
Glasgow	6 ,,	,,	11,000 ,,	4 ,,		,,	10,000 ,,
Scharnhorst	8.2 ,,	,,	13,500 ,,	5.9,,		,,	11,000 ,,
Leipzig	4.1 ,,	,,	11,500 ,,				

Personal opinion would undoubtedly have played a part in the compilation of the above table, but this is the most *optimistic* of all the tables which appear in the various writings upon this subject. In the Royal Naval Gunnery Establishment (H.M.S. *Excellent*) there is a deposition by a gunnery officer who was aboard *Canopus* at the time, which roundly affirms that the maximum effective range of her 12-inch guns in 1914 was only 9,000 yards under good conditions, and in the conditions which obtained at Coronel the range would only have been 4,000 yards. Even at this range, there is no reason to believe that her gunnery would have been any better than that of *Glasgow*, the only British ship present at the battle manned by long-service officers and men, so von Spee could well have fought his battle by the same tactics, and still have won it.

But from Cradock's point of view it was not the gunnery of *Canopus* which mattered so much as her speed. *In his experience*, her engines were defective and she could not steam at more than twelve and a half knots—and the fact that she made fifteen knots that very afternoon in a frantic effort to reach the battle area (aided by a following sea and a wind of gale strength) is immaterial. Cradock was never to know that.

What he did know was that if he followed the tactics which his critics state was the correct one, enticing the German squadron south to meet *Canopus*, he might well be placed in the dreadful position of having to watch the enemy circle to westwards and past him, whilst he was tied to a heavy ship whose engines might well have broken down yet again. True, should this happen, von Spee would undoubtedly have to stop before reaching the Horn in order to coal—but where? The German Admiral had evidently already mastered the enormous fuel problem entailed in crossing the Pacific, and in view of the sympathies of the Chilean Government and people, it was quite possible that his bunkers had been filled the previous day, and that colliers were awaiting him at hundred mile intervals along any one of fifty sea-routes between Coronel and the Cape.

And around the Horn, like a plum for the picking, awaited the main British base and coaling station in the South Atlantic, the virtually unprotected Falkland Islands (which incidentally constituted Cradock's only hope for further operations), while to the north lay the thronging trade lanes of the Plate upon whose inviolability depended the supply of much of Britain's war material and more of her food. There were ships of the Royal Navy under Admiral Stoddart operating north of Montevideo certainly, but until they had actually caught and annihilated the German ships (and from Cradock's latest intelligence they seemed only slightly better fitted to do this than those under his own command) von Spee could wreak dreadful havoc off the South American coast with catastrophic results upon England's war economy, and worse upon world opinion.

Nor was that all, for if von Spee, in addition to his presence in the South Atlantic, could explain it by announcing to the world that he had arrived there simply by steaming around a Royal Naval squadron too weak or pusillanimous to attack him, then Great Britain's prestige would indeed be utterly and irrevocably destroyed. No matter how swift the retribution meted out to the East Asiatic Squadron, it would never be forgotten that ships of the Royal Navy had refused a fleet action upon the first occasion that it was specifically offered after Trafalgar—nor that Kit Cradock had been in command.

That he—of all people—would have been the man to break tradition, would have been insupportable to Cradock. Like most

Englishmen, he made no particular show of his religion and was yet a religious man, and with an attitude of mind which is not untypical of our race, he had probably often thanked God humbly and sincerely for his nationality. He was undoubtedly grateful that Fate had chosen him to serve in the Royal Navy with sufficient distinction to bring him awards and promotions up to his present rank : an infinitesimal proportion of the world's populace fly their flags above the decks of British men-of-war, and Cradock was not unaware of the fact. He blessed his Fortune.

And on the afternoon of 1 November 1914, he may well have felt that he was being offered a crowning glory—for he was to be the first man to lead a squadron of the Royal Navy against an enemy fleet awaiting battle, for over a hundred years.

For—and he probably knew this exactly—one hundred and nine years and eleven days.

Since the day Nelson died.

Cradock could not have been aware that a choice of action existed for anyone to take, let alone himself. No matter how weak in comparison the British forces were, no matter how wise a retreat would have been or how smoothly and reasonably a withdrawal to the dubious protection of *Canopus* (at the expense of *Otranto*) could have been explained away, he could have had no choice.

Expect the sun to set in the east and water to run uphill, but not—in those circumstances—Kit Cradock to run from the enemy. For phrase it how you will, that is how he would have seen it.

As to the wisdom of his actual tactics, there have been interminable arguments. Had he been able to inflict anything more than purely superficial damage on the ships of von Spee's command, the German Admiral would undoubtedly have been in an exceedingly difficult position, for he was without bases or dockyard facilities with which to carry out repairs. As it was, the German ships used up a considerable proportion of their irreplaceable ammunition, and only a well-organized and well-directed clandestine system of colliers from supposedly neutral ports kept them in movement on the Pacific coast.

It has been suggested that once the two lines of battle had been formed, *Otranto* should have been ordered away and the three British cruisers driven forward during the time when the sun was in their favour. The German ships would have continued the retreat which they did in fact begin when Cradock initiated a similar move, and with the passing of time, *Otranto* would have been far enough away to render pursuit unlikely, and the cruisers could then have turned south towards *Canopus*.

But that—to Cradock—would still have been a retreat from the enemy.

So he stayed and fought—and died.

And no one who knew him could have expected anything else.

Of course, there is just as much to be said in support of the actions and decisions taken at the Admiralty. During the three months which had elapsed since the outbreak of war, the resources of the Royal Navy had been strained to the utmost. The great preponderance of Britain's naval strength was locked in the North Sea awaiting the appearance of the German High Seas Fleet, and the Homeric trial of strength which would surely then take place. In the Mediterranean British ships guarded the convoys of French Colonial troops against possible attack from Austrian naval units, from *Goeben* and her consort by then in the Bosphorus, and from the as yet unplumbed menace of the U-boat. In the Western Atlantic Royal Naval cruisers searched for the surface raider *Karlsruhe*, and an unknown (and as it happened, insignificant) number of armed merchantmen.

At first it had appeared as though the task of locating and annihilating the ships of von Spee's command would fall upon either or both the China and East Indies squadrons, but when Australia and New Zealand sprang to arms to assist Great Britain in her struggle, the emphasis changed. Now, instead of seeking out the enemy, the ships of these commands must protect the Anzac troop convoys against attack by them, and with the appearance early in September of *Emden* in the Bay of Bengal, that necessity had hardened. Admiral Jerram shifted his flag westwards from Hong Kong and hoisted it ashore at Singapore, leaving only a token force to assist the Japanese reduction of the German base at Tsingtao, and to protect British interests in the North Pacific.

To the south, steps were put in hand to make von Spee's position untenable by attacking German bases at Samoa and German New Guinea and occupying their territory. This of course made even more demands upon the naval forces, who now had to convoy these troopers and their provision ships as well.

As a result, to patrol and guard the sea routes stretching east and west from the South American continent, their Lordships had to rely upon what ships could be spared from the exiguous navies of the Commonwealth, a few ships of the Royal Navy which had been serving on southern stations and whom circumstances had not yet called home—and the ships of the Third Fleet, old, out of date and with their care and maintenance parties hastily made up to full complement with reservists, young cadets and boys.

In order to counter the threat which the East Asiatic Squadron constituted as it moved eastward across the Pacific, the Admiralty decided quite early to base a squadron of these ships on the Falkland Islands, and Admiral Cradock had been appointed to command it. The following telegram is the directive upon which he originally took up his duties.

From Admiralty to R-A. Good Hope, *via British Minister, Rio.* [Sent 14 September 1914, 5.50 p.m.]
There is a strong probability of the *Scharnhorst* and *Gneisenau* arriving in the Magellan Straits or on the west coast of South America.
The Germans have begun to carry on trade on the west coast of South America.
Leave sufficient force to deal with *Dresden* and *Karlsruhe*. Concentrate a squadron strong enough to meet *Scharnhorst* and *Gneisenau*, making Falkland Islands your coaling base. *Canopus* is now en route to Abrolhos. *Defence* is joining you from Mediterranean.
Until *Defence* joins, keep at least *Canopus* and one County class with your flagship. As soon as you have superior force, search the Magellan Straits with squadron, being ready to return and cover the River Plate,

or, according to information, search north as far as Valparaiso, break up the German trade and destroy the German cruisers.

Anchorage in the vicinity of Golfo Nuevo and Egg Harbour should be searched.

Colliers are being ordered to the Falkland Islands. Consider whether colliers from Abrolhos should be ordered south.

Abrolhos is a group of rocks (hardly islands) off the Brazilian coast. It should be noted that these original instructions included the order to destroy the German cruisers, and most important of all, that the modern armoured cruiser *Defence* was considered a necessary part of Cradock's strength. She carried four 9.2-inch guns and ten 7.5s, and in addition to her armour and gun-power, she had the inestimable advantage of youth, having been launched in 1907—the same year as *Scharnhorst*, and eight years later than *Canopus*. The comparative condition of her engines is patent.

However, shortly after these instructions were sent to Cradock it began to look instead as though von Spee contemplated an advance either into Australian waters or even towards the east coast of South Africa. With the menace to South American trade for the moment apparently dissolved, the Admiralty cancelled *Defence*'s orders and she remained in the Mediterranean, but possibly owing to difficulties of communication Cradock does not appear to have learned of this, and he spent his remaining time at Falklands wondering where on earth *Defence* had got to.

When, in October, von Spee's presence between the Marquesas and Easter Islands was again established and his move to the east confirmed, the following telegram was sent to Cradock at the Falkland Islands :

It appears from information received that *Gneisenau* and *Scharnhorst* are working across to South America. *Dresden* may be scouting for them. You must be prepared to meet them in company. *Canopus* should accompany *Glasgow*, *Monmouth* and *Otranto*, and should search and protect trade in combination.

The phrase 'search and protect trade' is one upon which the

33

critics of the Admiralty have made much play, but it is noteworthy that *Defence* was not mentioned. At the end of his reply to this telegram (dated 8 October) Cradock asked whether the armoured cruiser was to join his command or not, and in another telegram the same day, he made what might conceivably be construed as a strategic error. He pointed out to the Admiralty the possibility of von Spee eluding him on the west coast of South America, and the consequent advisability of having a second concentration of ships strong enough to meet the Germans in battle on the east coast as well. They should cruise sufficiently far south to catch von Spee as he rounded the Horn, and have at least a scouting cruiser off the entrance of the Magellan Straits to give warning of his arrival.

Perhaps the fault lay with Parliament and the British Electorate after all. The necessary warships did not apparently exist.

In a praiseworthy endeavour to fall in with the requirements of the commander on the spot, however, the Admiralty ordered *Defence* across the Atlantic again—but to join the flag of Admiral Stoddart, who was given control of the area north of Montevideo. Stoddart had as flagship the eleven-year-old cruiser *Carnarvon*, and in addition one County class cruiser like *Monmouth* and a light cruiser like *Glasgow* : with *Defence* his squadron was undoubtedly superior to Cradock's, but it is still doubtful if it would have been strong enough utterly to annihilate the German squadron—for that was what the situation would seem to have demanded.

The arrangement thus had the fatal weakness of compromise, and none of its occasional advantages. Concentrated, the two commands might have beaten the enemy, but not separately, and the completely inexplicable weakness was the power vacuum which would be left south of Montevideo once Cradock's force entered the Pacific. But it should be borne in mind that it was Cradock's prompting which initiated the formation of the two forces.

On 14 October, the Admiralty telegraphed Cradock to inform him of these arrangements, and on the 18th, he replied as follows :

I consider it possible that *Karlsruhe* has been driven west, and is to join the other five [i.e., von Spee's squadron]. I trust circumstances will enable me to force an action, but fear that strategically, owing to *Canopus*, the speed of my squadron cannot exceed 12 knots.

Here we have the fundamental misunderstanding, for Churchill quotes this telegram in *The World Crisis*, following it with the comment:

> Thus it is clear that up to this date the Admiral fully intended to keep concentrated on the *Canopus*, even though his squadron speed should be reduced to 12 knots.

This would undoubtedly have been the intention and attitude behind such a despatch if sent by Wellington—'If I can't win, I don't fight'—and it probably never dawned upon the First Lord that Cradock's cable contained an ambiguity. It revealed the alternative of either fighting *without* the guns of *Canopus*, or remaining under their dubious protection and thus possibly allowing the enemy to steam past unmolested. No one pointed out to Mr Churchill that Cradock would regard the second alternative as unacceptable as he himself regarded the first; in fact, further communications and memoranda were to a great extent to confirm to Churchill that his reading of the situation was correct.

On 26 October, Cradock sent another telegram to the Admiralty:

Rear-Admiral Cradock to Admiralty. Good Hope. 26 *October*. *At sea*. Admiralty telegram received 7th October [i.e. the 'search and protect' telegram]. With reference to orders to search for the enemy and our great desire for early success, I consider that owing to slow speed of *Canopus* it is impossible to find and destroy enemy's squadron.
Have therefore ordered *Defence* to join me after calling for orders at Montevideo.
Shall employ *Canopus* on necessary work of convoying colliers.

Here possibly was an occasion for the misunderstandings to be cleared away, but tragically, the telegram arrived at a time of turmoil at Whitehall. In the middle of many disturbances and distractions, Mr Churchill annotated the telegram to the effect that he found it very obscure and that he was not certain what Admiral Cradock either intended or wished. He forwarded it to his Naval Secretary for elucidation and it was returned with the following reply :

> The situation on the west coast seems safe. If *Gneisenau* and *Scharnhorst* have gone north they will meet eventually *Idzumo*, *Newcastle* and *Hizen* [the first and last were Japanese warships] moving south, and will be forced south on *Glasgow* and *Monmouth* who have good speed and can keep touch and draw them south on to *Good Hope* and *Canopus*, who should keep within supporting distance of each other.

It would not have been up to Mr Churchill to question the opinions of his technical experts, even had they disagreed with his own, but it is one of our national tragedies that the writer of one memorandum now in the Admiralty files was not sufficiently senior in rank for his opinions to merit the consideration which— in this instance at least—they deserved. Captain (later Admiral) Herbert Richmond had held the appointment of Assistant Director of Naval Operations since February 1913, and his appreciation of the situation in South American waters at this time contains the following passage :

> They [the ships under Cradock's command] are not capable of preventing harm being done because—
> 1.   They are too slow if they act together.
> 2.   Their armaments are not superior to the Germans'.
> 3.   Their crews are new and their gunnery is not likely to be of as high a standard as the Germans'—the ships being two months in commission against over a year of the enemy.
> 4.   If the Germans consider themselves superior, they can engage these ships : if they do not think an engagement worth risking in view of more important operations ... they can round the Horn and avoid falling in with the British ships.

When this appreciation reached Mr Churchill, he referred it

(with the author's consent—indeed recommendation) once more to his Naval Secretary, but unfortunately this interchange between assistants was really at too low a level for such a vital matter. Richmond's direct superior was not in agreement with the views expressed in the appreciation, and neither was the Chief of Staff, Vice-Admiral Sir Doveton Sturdee, and whatever the opinions of Churchill himself or his Naval Secretary, the First Lord of the Admiralty did not feel that in the peculiar and tragic circumstances which attended the last fortnight of October 1914 he could place yet more burdens on the shoulders of the man who should have been his highest technical adviser. So he turned to people who had neither the experience, nor indeed the rank or responsibility to give it. The Naval Secretary and the other officers consulted gave their opinions with complete sincerity and with all the knowledge they possessed.

But at any other time of the war there would have been a higher authority to whom the matter could have been referred.

CHAPTER FOUR

THE appointment which Mr Churchill held at the outbreak of the war—that of First Lord of the Admiralty—is of course a Cabinet post occupied as such by a politician, not a seaman. The senior executive officer of the Royal Navy, with whom the First Lord must work in harmony and close collaboration, is the First Sea Lord, and at that time this position was held by Admiral Prince Louis of Battenberg, an officer of long sea experience and great distinction of mind and manner, who had been a naturalized British subject since his fourteenth year.

His life had been spent in the service of the Royal Navy and of England, and it is worth noting that his brother had died of yellow fever contracted whilst serving with the British Army during the Ashanti war, and his nephew Prince Maurice was killed on the Western Front during the retreat from Antwerp. When upon a visit to Kiel at the beginning of the century, Prince Louis had been reproached by a German Admiral for serving with the British Navy, he pointed out coldly that he was an Englishman, and that in any case, when he joined the Royal Navy, neither the German Empire nor the Imperial Navy had been even in existence.

But he *had* been born in Germany and he was the son of a German Prince—Alexander of Hesse. This was the basic foundation upon which many interested parties were to raise a structure of slander and deceit—and doubtless the German Intelligence Services were only too willing to co-operate in the downfall of a highly efficient senior officer of the British Crown. They were aided by events. After the minor disasters of the opening weeks of the war—the escape of *Goeben* and *Breslau* through the Dardanelles, the loss of *Pathfinder*, the early successes of *Emden* and *Karlsruhe*—it was only too easy to sow suspicion in the minds of the public, already febrile with spy mania and totally incapable of seeing the woods of overall but static naval success, for the trees of comparatively insignificant, but violent and thus conspicuous, local disaster.

The suspicions were cultivated and the distrust grew—and a sensitive, civilized and honourable man, whilst endeavouring to shoulder the enormous burden of responsibilities which his post entailed, was made fully aware that his position was being steadily undermined. The task of fulfilling the duties of First Sea Lord is one which has broken the health of strong men in peacetime : during a war it demands the concentrated attention of body, brain and spirit which only freedom from other commitments and distractions and an atmosphere of trust and confidence can engender.

These essential conditions Prince Louis was denied.

On 22 September, *Aboukir*, *Hogue* and *Cressy* were torpedoed in the North Sea. Public outcry was at first broad and general in its criticism of the Admiralty as a whole, but with a little judicious direction it soon found its focus. Articles appeared in the less reputable newspapers upon the subject of the First Sea Lord's ancestry and family connections. His immense services to England were forgotten and those who would have most indignantly denied the rumours and countered the lies—the men of the Royal Navy —were penned aboard their ships at sea.

And then Prince Louis was subjected to the infinite malice of the anonymous letter-writer. This was no straw to break a camel's back—it was the ultimate weapon of a despicable campaign to drive a faithful servant from office.

But it took time.

It took the whole of the month of October 1914, and during those fateful days when Cradock was awaiting reinforcements with which to annihilate von Spee, and Mr Churchill was misunderstanding his intention and sending him the possible means of a protection he did not want, the man with the rank and responsibility to clarify the whole matter and rectify the mistakes, was suffering the agony of mind which only accumulated spite can inflict.

To say that the First Sea Lord should have ignored the attacks upon him is fatuous—as well expect a surgeon to operate with a splinter under his nail and grit in his eye. But he carried on until it was obvious that his position was being made untenable.

Prince Louis resigned his office as First Sea Lord on 29 October —when *Glasgow* was off Coronel, *Otranto* was making for Puerto Montt, *Good Hope* and *Monmouth* were at Vallenar and *Canopus* was labouring up from the Magellan Straits. It was already too late to intervene, but in any assessment of responsibility for what was so soon to happen, it might be as well to take into account the part played by those who combined—knowingly or unknowingly —to hound a fine sailor and great patriot from an office which he was filling with great efficiency and greater distinction.

In order to ensure that there should be no untoward break in the work of the Navy, Prince Louis had informed Sir John Jellicoe of his intention to resign, whereupon the Commander-in-Chief addressed the following telegram to him :

Have received with the most profound sorrow the information contained in your telegram. The whole Fleet will learn the news when published with the deepest possible regret. We look to you with the greatest loyalty, respect and gratitude for the work you have accomplished for the Navy.

It is to be hoped that these words offered some degree of comfort to Prince Louis during the months of heart-breaking disappointment which lay ahead.

But the Navy's task is continual, and its highest office cannot remain vacant for long. On the day after Prince Louis's resignation, that startling and ferocious old man, Lord Fisher, returned to the Admiralty in order to re-occupy the position of First Sea Lord, which he had already held from 1904 to 1910.

During Fisher's career the Royal Navy had been completely transformed—and a great deal of the transformation was due to him. To him has been accorded the responsibility for the introduction of the water-tube boiler, the submarine, the Dreadnought, the common education scheme, the system of nucleus crews for ships in reserve, the great naval building programmes of the early years of this century, and the concentration of the Fleets in home waters. He was the first to encourage the step from the 12-inch to the 13.5-inch gun and as soon as it proved practicable he rushed ahead with plans for the 15-inch gun.

His energy was phenomenal, and that his success matched it was due to his force of will and his complete ruthlessness. He has often been called a genius, and certainly the astounding achievements accredited to him seem to bear out the claim, and so do the stories of his vindictiveness, his deep undying hatreds, the schisms his violence instigated, and the intrigues by which he sought to ruin those who stood in his way—for genius has its darker side.

It seems to have been imposssible to have had an honest difference of opinion with Fisher. If it could not be seen—immediately and with his own blinding clarity—that what he proposed was the only correct course, if there was hesitation or obstruction, it could not be through a genuine misunderstanding but only through some devious and ulterior motive. Disagreement with him therefore—in his eyes—was never even stupidity or blindness, it was a crime against the country and the Service, and as such, its instigators must be eliminated.

The age-long feud which raged between Fisher and Lord Charles Beresford in the 1900s, had split the Service from top to bottom, and when Fisher went in 1910, the Navy drew a sigh of relief. But in the circumstances which so tragically developed, it is not surprising that they drew another when they heard he was back.

Mr Churchill has described his return to the Admiralty.

As soon as he entered the Admiralty I took him to the War Room and went over with him on the great map the positions and tasks of every vessel in our immense organization. It took more than two hours. The critical point was clearly in South American waters. Speaking of Admiral Cradock's position, I said, 'You don't suppose he would try to fight them without the *Canopus*?'

He did not give any decided reply.

This must be one of the few instances of Lord Fisher failing to respond immediately and violently to a presented situation. Presumably his mind was too full of the enormous complexity of the overall task with which he was confronted, for a weakness in a comparatively minor field to engage his full concentration, but it has been suggested that he was silent because he foresaw exactly what Cradock would do—and would indeed have had him court-martialled had he done anything else, for it is surely unlikely that Fisher would have retreated from von Spee any more than did Cradock.

And knowing rather more about Mr Churchill now than possibly he did about himself in those days, we are entitled to wonder how *he* would have reacted had *he* stood in Cradock's shoes. It seems unlikely that he would have won for himself a reputation for caution then, any more than he has done throughout the rest of his tumultuous life.

On 3 November, a telegram was received from His Majesty's Consul-General at Valparaiso to the effect that the German squadron had been seen off the coast on the morning of 1 November. One of Fisher's first acts after taking office was thus to send telegrams ordering the *Defence* around the Horn to Cradock's support and to the Japanese Government suggesting that their heavy squadrons move east and south to close in upon the enemy. Also the following :

To R-A. Good Hope. 3 *November*, 6.55 *p.m.*
Defence has been ordered to join your flag with all dispatch. *Glasgow* should find or keep in touch with the enemy. You should keep touch with *Glasgow* concentrating the rest of your squadron including *Canopus*.

It is important you should effect your junction with *Defence* at earliest possible moment subject to keeping touch with *Glasgow* and enemy. Enemy supposes you at Corcovado Bay. Acknowledge.

Alas, the enemy by then knew exactly where Cradock and his men were, and there was no acknowledgement. The Admiralty were talking to a void.

At seven o'clock the following morning Mr Churchill opened the telegram which gave first intimation of the disaster at Coronel. Despite a cautious and doubtful press release which was issued by the Admiralty, it seems that both the First Lord and the First Sea Lord acted immediately upon the assumption that the information contained in the telegram was correct. By ten o'clock the Operations Division were already ferreting out the answers to a truly Churchillian demand :

Director of Operations Division.   4/11/14
1. How far is it, and how long would it take *Dartmouth* and *Weymouth* to reach Punta Arenas, Rio or Abrolhos respectively, if they started this afternoon with all dispatch?
2. How long would it take—
    a. *Kent* to reach Rio and Abrolhos?
    b. *Australia* (i) without, and (ii) with *Montcalm* to reach Galapagos via Makada Islands, and also *Idzumo* and *Newcastle* to reach them?
    c. The Japanese 2nd Southern Squadron to replace *Australia* at Fiji?
    d. *Defence*, *Carnarvon* and *Cornwall* respectively to reach Punta Arenas?
    e. *Invincible* to reach Abrolhos, Rio, Punta Arenas?
    f. *Hizen* and *Asama* to reach Galapagos or Esquimalt?
                                                                         W.S.C.

It was obvious that the First Lord meant business and that he would attend conference well-briefed should technical reasons be advanced for delaying action. There was some speculation upon the results of an immediate head-on collision between the civil and Service chiefs—and even Churchill must have wondered how his new First Sea Lord would react to the idea of reducing the strength of the Grand Fleet by the striking power of the battle-cruiser *Invincible*.

He need not have worried. Lord Fisher had spent his life dealing with crises and had learned years before that one cannot win a war without taking risks. The proposed re-shuffle of armoured and un-armoured cruisers interested him not at all. *Three* battle-cruisers must immediately be released for service in the Atlantic—two to go far south to the Falklands and one to the West Indies in case von Spee should move north and come through the Panama Canal. There was to be no more doubt in anyone's mind, no more mis-understandings, no more attempts to contain a strong, concentrated force within a weak, attenuated line. Von Spee was to be hunted, found and annihilated, and the necessary re-deployment was to be carried out with true Fisherite energy and dispatch.

The following telegram was sent north to Sir John Jellicoe, Commander-in-Chief of the Grand Fleet :

Order *Invincible* and *Inflexible* to fill up with coal at once and proceed to Berehaven with all dispatch. They are urgently needed for foreign service. Admiral and Flag Captain *Invincible* to transfer to *New Zealand*. Captain *New Zealand* to *Invincible*. . . .

It is interesting to note that Churchill considered it polite—or perhaps even politic—to send a further telegram to the C.-in-C., couched in rather less stringent terms and containing a modicum of explanation, but whether it was necessary or not, Sir John parted with his battle-cruisers without a word and as they were in some need of dockyard attention, they steamed down the west coast of Ireland to Devonport, where work was immediately commenced upon them at high pressure.

But the ordering away of the battle-cruisers was only a part of the plan. 'Destroy opposition with overwhelming force' was another of Fisher's doctrines, 'wherever it presents itself', and there were quite a number of alternative courses of action which von Spee might follow, and which must be forestalled.

The German Admiral might, for instance, break back across the Pacific—so the Japanese 1st Southern Squadron, consisting of a battleship, two battle-cruisers and two light cruisers and supported by *Montcalm* and *Encounter*, were ordered to spread out from Suva to meet him, while to the north *Australia*, *Newcastle*, *Hizen* and *Idzumo* were to lie in wait. Should von Spee reach the Pacific entrance to the Panama Canal and pass through it, he would meet the battle-cruiser *Princess Royal* in the Caribbean, together with the cruisers *Condé*, *Berwick* and *Lancaster*.

And if he followed *Glasgow* and *Canopus* around the Horn into the Atlantic, he would enter Admiral Stoddart's area of command whose force was now combined to contain him. *Glasgow* and *Canopus* were ordered north to join Stoddart's flag, and by 12 November *Glasgow*, *Carnarvon*, *Defence*, *Cornwall* and the armed merchantmen *Otranto* and *Orama*, were patrolling off Montevideo. Even so, Admiral Stoddart had orders that he was not to engage the enemy until the battle-cruisers arrived. He was only to shadow them.

Canopus had left Falkland Islands at the same time as *Glasgow* under orders to join Stoddart's flag with her, but at last the state of her engines was appreciated and the Admiral ordered her back to Stanley Harbour as guardship. In order to guard the southern approaches to Port William and the main anchorages, Captain Grant took his ship through the outer bay and into the landlocked harbour itself, and finding that anchors and warps would not hold him in the position required, he grounded *Canopus* so that her broadside would fire over a low neck of land and into the required beaten zone. The upper works of the ship were daubed all colours of the rainbow, an observation and gunnery-control post was set up, twelve-pounder guns sent ashore and mounted in three batteries, and the local volunteers drilled in anti-invasion tactics. Slabs of gun-cotton were inserted underneath the more useful dockyard installations and oil-soaked waste piled among the coal-dumps. The island was certainly not to be abandoned—but it might fall.

The reflection crossed the mind of one Admiralty official that if von Spee was to learn of all this he would undoubtedly have cause for apprehension—but also for considerable satisfaction. Not many units of the Imperial German Navy have engaged the full attention of five times their own numerical strength.

Back in England, *Invincible* and *Inflexible* had arrived at Devonport on the morning of Sunday, 8 November, and on 9 November the following message reached the Admiralty :

The Admiral Superintendent, Devonport, reports that the earliest possible date for completion of *Invincible* and *Inflexible* is midnight 13 November.

There have been times in the history of the Admiralty when such an announcement would have been accepted with the reflection that what would be, would be—and if anyone felt superstitious about Friday the 13th, then the sailing had better be put back to Saturday the 14th.

But not now.

Lord Fisher was with Mr Churchill at the time of arrival of the message, and within an hour the Admiral Superintendent was reading their reply.

Admiralty to C.-in-C. Devonport.
Ships are to sail Wednesday 11th. They are needed for war service and dockyard arrangements must be made to conform. If necessary dockyard men should be sent away in the ships to return as opportunity may offer. You are held responsible for the speedy despatch of these ships in a thoroughly efficient condition. Acknowledge.

W.S.C.

Invincible and *Inflexible* sailed at 6 p.m. on Wednesday.
Lord Fisher was back indeed.

Flying his flag on *Invincible* and in command of the squadron went Vice-Admiral Sir Frederick Doveton Sturdee. Few naval officers have ever been given such wide powers, such a precise and unmistakable objective and such overwhelming strength with which to attain it. His command covered the South Pacific and South Atlantic—and if his quarry should make it necessary, every other waterway upon which his ships would sail. His objective was the annihilation of von Spee's squadron, and ships of other Admirals, should he enter their areas of command, were to be placed at his disposal. He commanded an avenging force so large as to make victory a virtual certainty.

An investigation of the circumstances in which he came to occupy such a thoroughly enviable position produces a curious picture.

Until the day before he hoisted his flag on *Invincible*, Sturdee had been Chief of Staff at the Admiralty—and it has been suggested that as he bore some share in the responsibility for the Coronel disaster, he had been given command in order to make amends. This is unlikely, for the Admiralty does not reward even suspected inefficiency in administration with high executive command. It wishes to stay in business.

In the portion of Churchill's *The World Crisis* which deals with this aspect of affairs occurs the following passage :

> In Admiral Sturdee the Navy had a sea officer of keen intelligence and great practical ability—a man who could handle and fight his ship or his squadron with the utmost skill and resolution. But he was not a man with whom Lord Fisher could have worked satisfactorily at the supreme administrative centre.

Now whatever can be (and has been) said against Lord Fisher, it has never been seriously suggested that he surrounded himself merely with fawning courtiers. Neither flattery nor sycophancy succeeded with him. What he demanded was wholehearted accordance with his plans and the ability and determination necessary to turn them into reality. His egotism however, ruled that whoever was not for him was implacably against him, and an examination of Sturdee's career reveals a most significant fact. From 1905 to 1907 he had been Chief of Staff in the Mediterranean Fleet, following it with a similar appointment in the Channel Fleet. On both stations his Commander-in-Chief had been Lord Charles Beresford.

Not every member, apparently, of the anti-Fisher coalition was doomed, although the whole business may provide an example of the ruthlessness which cleared his opponents (or even possible critics) from Lord Fisher's immediate vicinity. Up or down did not matter as long as they went, but it will be seen that in these circumstances Admiral Sturdee's command was by no means an unmixed blessing. Although his powers were wide, so were the oceans —and unless the intelligence organization at work in the southern hemisphere could provide him with rather better service than they had given to Admiral Cradock, then von Spee might easily elude his battle-cruisers, and either reach the Fatherland (if such was his objective) or else be brought to book by some Flag Officer standing perhaps higher in Lord Fisher's estimation than Admiral Sturdee did. The prospect of the obloquy which the First Sea Lord would then bring down upon his head must have caused the Admiral some deep and anxious thought during the next few weeks.

The first leg of the journey took the battle-cruisers to St Vincent, Cape Verde, where they coaled and were of course seen by a large number of people. One of them at least must have been a cable operator, for on 17 November, Lieutenant Hirst—still Intelligence Officer to the South Atlantic Fleet—whilst lunching at the Club Central in Rio de Janeiro, overheard two Englishmen discussing the imminent arrival of *Invincible* and *Inflexible* in southern waters. As two Germans were sitting only a few tables away the situation had to be handled delicately, but Hirst eventually traced the leakage to the Western Union Telegraph and the Superintendent was approached. He did what he could to stem the rumours, but it seems that the German Intelligence centre at La Plata did pick up the information, and decided to send it down to a collier rendezvous with Admiral von Spee at Port Santa Elena on the Patagonian coast.

Already some of Sturdee's advantages in power and weight were being placed in jeopardy by human factors.

On 26 November, the battle-cruisers reached Abrolhos Rocks to find awaiting them there, *Glasgow* (rejuvenated after a spell in the dry dock at Rio), *Defence*, *Carnarvon*, *Cornwall*, *Bristol*, *Kent*, a host of colliers, and the armed merchantman *Orama* (*Otranto* had been packed off to Sierra Leone for boiler examination). While the stores brought out for the light cruisers were being distributed, and all ships were coaling, Admiral Sturdee called conferences of the senior officers to discuss the situation and to draw up plans for the search for, and elimination of, the East Asiatic Squadron.

Aboard *Inflexible* as First and Gunnery Lieutenant was Lieutenant-Commander Rudolph Verner, R.N., a brilliant and promising young officer. On the day after the arrival at Abrolhos, he wrote in a letter to his father

> ... As usual when I write to you I am d——d tired, just finished coaling, 1,800 tons. Temperature 100 degrees in the shade, and off again tomorrow.
>
> Had much information re action off Valparaiso. It was as I thought. An English Admiral manœuvred into a hopeless position from which he *could* have extricated himself, refused to do so since 'he would rather burst than let a damned scoundrel of a German etc., etc.'

This is interesting, in that the quotation which Verner paraphrased is one of Nelson's, who annnounced to a Colonel of the Rifle Brigade (then the 95th Rifles) : 'For myself, I would rather burst than let a damned rascal of a Frenchman know that peace or war affected me with either joy or sorrow.'

Cradock, one feels, would have been much gratified could he have seen the young man's letter.

On 28 November, at 10 a.m., the entire squadron sailed south. As a result of the conferences and what meagre information could be gathered, Admiral Sturdee concluded that although von Spee might well be around the Horn (one report suggested this, but the reliability of the source was in doubt) the ships of his command should at least reach the trade lanes from the Plate before the Germans. The Falklands must surely be a tempting bait for von Spee, and as a routine signal was received from the wireless station there every morning it seemed that the German squadron was not yet in that vicinity.

Nevertheless, the sooner the British ships were at Port Stanley, the sooner some of the general obscurity of the situation might be cleared away.

Spread out to the maximum distance which would still allow visual communication along the line, the squadron moved south in line abreast. Only searchlights were to be used for signalling purposes and wireless traffic was expressly forbidden. The battle-cruisers were grouped in the centre for quick concentration, the cruisers and light cruisers out on either wing. *Orama* shepherded the colliers along in the rear. By 3 December, the *Macedonia* had joined the line, the squadron was down past Rio Grande do Sul and the thermometer falling steadily; on 5 December, a beam sea brought an uncomfortable reminder that in those seas December is the worst month for gales.

A little more information had come to hand—for what it was worth. Two German steamers were reported to have left the Plate with coal aboard, and one loaded with provisions had left Monte-video. It looked as though von Spee might well have rounded the Horn, but by this time a rebellion in South Africa under the Boer leader de Wet was gaining prominence in world headlines. As it happened the press was late for the rebellion had practically been crushed by this time, but von Spee was not to know this and the situation posed the question as to whether the Asiatic Squadron was coming up the Atlantic towards the British squadron, or whether it was crossing their front towards the Cape of Good Hope to assist the rebellion. Sturdee during this time must have felt the full weight of his responsibilities.

On 7 December, the Falkland Islands were at last sighted and the squadron was ordered to concentrate in Stanley Harbour or the outer bay at Port William, for coaling. Some of the ships were by now in need of more attention than the mere filling of their bunkers—*Bristol* and *Cornwall*, for instance, must be allowed to draw their fires for boiler examination and overhaul—but it was essential that no time whatever should be lost. *Macedonia* was posted outside the line of improvised mines which Captain Heath-cote Grant had strung across the entrance to the bay and the light cruiser *Kent* patrolled just inside the line. *Glasgow* and *Carnarvon* coaled straight on through the night from the only two colliers as yet available (*Orama* and her colliers were days astern), and at daybreak the colliers left them and went alongside the battle-cruisers to begin fulfilling their enormous coal demands.

This question of coal supplies and coaling operations was undoubtedly the most important secondary problem which faced Sturdee. It was difficult enough to arrange matters during wartime when merely a journey between two points was envisaged—especially for a squadron the size of the one now under his command. Tomorrow, or at the latest the day after, his ships would be out sweeping the seas for an elusive foe—and there is no pastime more expensive in energy (or in this case fuel) than looking for a needle in a haystack, especially if one has a choice of haystacks. The problem of coal supplies, if his ships had to search either beyond the Horn or towards Table Bay, could become so complex as to be virtually insuperable—and in the absence of good luck, the German ships might easily be sighted and then lost again because of it.

Not that this would be accepted in Whitehall as an excuse. No excuse would be accepted for failure in any form, and Admiral Sturdee knew it : his head on a charger would be the least that Lord Fisher would demand should von Spee elude his battle-cruisers.

And at the conference of ships' captains which the Admiral called upon the evening of 7 December, it was only too obvious that there was still a woeful lack of information regarding the enemy's position or even his movements since Coronel. Two days before, reliable information had come in that the German armed merchantman *Prinz Eitel Friedrich* was still at Valparaiso—but this was the type of news item which might mean everything, or nothing. It was known that this ship had been in company with von Spee during the journey across the Pacific, but whether she was now on permanent detachment, or still in close contact with the Admiral, was not known.

Where was von Spee now? That was the main problem.

What had he been doing and where had he been hiding himself since his victory at Coronel?

CHAPTER FIVE

It is not unduly difficult, forty-five years after the events, to trace the movements of the East Asiatic Squadron subsequent to the action off Coronel. Neither is it impossible to find and examine copies of the signals containing information or instructions which Admiral von Spee received from Berlin, his own replies, or the telegrams he sent to the German agencies in the Americas and West Africa.

What, however, will always remain matters of conjecture are the reasons for the actions which he took and the processes of thought which led to the decisions he made.

In the following pages an attempt has been made to reconstruct a coherent picture of the situation which developed in South American waters between 1 November and 7 December 1914. The observed and recorded events are by now matters of history, and they of course dictate the main shape of the picture. In addition, background colour is provided by the memoranda written by von Spee in the course of his naval career and especially after his appointment as Commander-in-Chief at Tsingtao, and some of the foreground detail, too—his orders to subordinate officers, his verbal comments and remarks to those about him—are recorded fact.

But those passages dealing with von Spee's innermost thoughts, with what went on in his mind, are the result of surmise on the part of the writer, arrived at after close study of the man, his career and his writing. It is believed that they fit the known events.

It is hoped that they help to present a rational account of what took place.

*   *   *

As the waves had at last closed above *Monmouth*'s stern upon that grim, storm-wracked evening off Coronel, *Nürnberg*'s lookouts saw in the moonlight two columns of smoke pass, and then apparently re-pass, between themselves and the coast. The seas were too high for rescue work, however great may have been the wish to save life, and here in any case might be the primary target of all warships, an enemy unit. Captain von Schönberg therefore, ordered a course towards the smoke, and *Nürnberg* left the scene of her late infelicitous triumph.

By 9.30 p.m. the smoke columns had been found to emanate from the *Scharnhorst*'s funnels; *Nürnberg* rejoined the flag at last and by ten o'clock the ships of von Spee's command were all sweeping slowly in line abreast over the heaving seas, crossing and criss-crossing in search of the remainder of Admiral Cradock's squadron. As night passed, the wind fell and the waves moderated. Dawn revealed a calming, empty sea under the clear skies.

They turned together once more, then in response to signals fluttering from *Scharnhorst*'s halliards, the light cruisers formed line ahead parallel to the coast and moving north, while the armoured cruisers came steadily up between them and the land. In the clear, refreshing light all doubts evaporated and regrets were blown away on the crisp invigorating breeze, and as *Scharnhorst* came abreast of each ship the crews cheered their Admiral, each other, themselves, the battle. From *Scharnhorst* came the acknowledgement : 'By the Grace of God a fine victory. My thanks and good wishes to the crews.'

The sun rose, the watches changed, the morning warmed.

In his day cabin, the Commander-in-Chief sat at his desk, writing the interminable signals, the telegrams, the War Diary, the Naval Staff reports.

Then he wrote a letter.

Yesterday was All Saints' Day and a lucky day for us. I was steaming south along the coast with the squadron when I received information that a British cruiser had run into Coronel, a small coaling station near Concepcion. As according to International Law a belligerent vessel must leave again within twenty-four hours, I thought of catching her. In the dispositions I then made, *Nürnberg* was to steam past the entrance to see if the cruiser was still there, while the remaining ships were placed in a semi-circle outside. To economize coal the ships had only steam for fourteen knots but were ready to develop their full boiler-power at short notice.

My ships were therefore somewhat scattered, *Gneisenau* alone being quite close, when at 4.25 p.m. it was reported to me that two ships had been sighted to the south-west. I headed for them and ordered the other ships to join me as it was soon clear that they were enemy ships—none other than the armoured cruiser *Monmouth* and the light cruiser *Glasgow*. Soon afterwards we sighted astern of them the armed merchant cruiser *Otranto* and a little later the armoured cruiser *Good Hope*.

The enemy tried various movements which would have brought him nearer to the coast and to windward of me, which would have been bad for us. I had at once ordered *Scharnhorst* and *Gneisenau* to raise steam for full speed and in quarter of an hour we were steaming twenty knots against a heavy sea, which fortunately enabled us to get on a parallel course with the enemy—but we were alone and had to wait for the others. The enemy were amiable enough not to disturb us in this.

We were then about nine miles apart. As soon as my ships—except *Nürnberg*, not yet in sight—were collected, I began at 6.10 p.m. to decrease the distance, and when we were five miles apart I opened fire. The action had begun, and generally speaking I led the line steadily with few alterations of course. I had outmanoeuvred the sun in the west so that he could no longer hinder me; the moon in the east was not yet full but promised to shine well in the night. Rain squalls were to be seen here and there. My ships fired rapidly and with good effect on the big enemy ships. *Scharnhorst* fired at *Good Hope*—flagship of Admiral Cradock, *Gneisenau* at *Monmouth*, *Leipzig* at *Glasgow*, *Dresden* at *Otranto*. The latter had quitted the line after a while and I think escaped.

On board *Good Hope* and *Monmouth* many fires broke out. A tremendous explosion occurred in the former, which looked like gigantic fire-works against the dark evening sky—white flames with green stars reaching higher than the funnels. I thought the ship would founder but the battle continued uninterruptedly.

Darkness came on.

I had reduced the distance at first to 4,500 metres, then I turned slowly away, increasing the distance again. Fire was continued against the ships made visible by the fires burning on board, but ceased when the gun-layers were no longer able to sight their guns.

The enemy's fire had ceased. I therefore ordered the light cruisers to continue in chase, but as the enemy had apparently extinguished his fires nothing was to be seen, and steaming around the hostile line in order to get a better light on it did not get another meeting. The action had lasted fifty-two minutes.

At 8.40 p.m. when steering north-west, we observed gun-fire ahead at a great distance, estimated at ten miles. I steered for it to render assis-tance if necessary. It turned out to be *Nürnberg* which had been unable to find me and now had come across *Monmouth*.

Nürnberg closed her and finished her off with her guns. *Monmouth* capsized and sank. Unfortunately the heavy sea forbade all attempts at saving life, apart from the fact that *Nürnberg* thought that she saw *Good Hope* not far off, which however, was probably a mistake. She may have taken one of our big cruisers in the moonlight at a distance, for her. I do not know what became of *Good Hope*. Lieutenant G—— who had leisure for observations, thinks he made out that she had a heavy list. Now I recall to mind what I saw, this appears quite possible, although I thought it was due to the movement of the ship in the heavy seas. It is possible that she also foundered—she was certainly *hors de combat*.

Glasgow we could hardly make out. It is believed that we got several hits on her, but in my opinion she escaped.

We have thus been victorious all along the line and I thank God we have suffered no losses. *Gneisenau* had a few cases of lightly wounded, our light cruisers were not hit at all. Such hits as *Gneisenau* and *Scharn-horst* received hardly caused any damage. A six-inch shell was found in one of the store-rooms of the *Scharnhorst*—it had come through the ship's side, made all kinds of havoc below but luckily did not burst and now lay there to greet us. One funnel was hit but not so as to prevent it continuing its function. Similar trivialities occurred in *Gneisenau*.

I know not what adverse circumstances deprived the enemy of every measure of success. The enthusiasm of our brave lads was tremendous, I could see how certain they were of victory and I am especially glad that *Nürnberg*, who through no fault of her own missed the battle, after all contributed to our success.

If *Good Hope* escapes she must in my opinion make for a Chilean port on account of her damage. To make sure of this I intend going to Valparaiso tomorrow with *Scharnhorst* and *Gneisenau* and to see whether *Good Hope* could not be disarmed by the Chileans. If so, I shall be relieved of two powerful opponents.

Good Hope, though bigger than *Scharnhorst*, was not so well armed. She mounted heavy guns, but only two—while *Monmouth* succumbed to *Gneisenau* as she had only 6-inch guns. The English have another ship like *Monmouth* hereabouts and in addition as it seems, a battleship of the Queen class carrying 12-inch guns. Against the latter we can hardly do anything—had they kept their force together we should probably have got the worst of it.

You can hardly imagine the joy which reigns among us. We have at last contributed something to the glory of our arms—although it might not mean much on the whole and in view of the enormous number of the English ships.

He read the letter through again, made minor alterations, added felicitations and good wishes, then signed it—his black incisive signature like a brooch on a white dress.

There, he thought—that should satisfy them. It would undoubtedly be read by many eyes other than those to whom it was addressed and would quite possibly reach the pages of the national press—a body for whom he did not have a great deal of appreciation in the normal way, but which he might as well make use of when convenient. It might serve to quieten the criticisms which were most probably being directed at him from behind the conference tables in Wilhelmstrasse.

He pushed back the chair, a tall, strongly-built, handsome man, carrying his fifty-three years with dignity, although with not quite so much ease as had been the case four months before. The furrows which bracketed the white moustache and clipped beard were deeper now, and new lines had etched themselves about the shrewd, marbled eyes.

It was time to take stock. What *had* his squadron done? What—
and he knew precisely the important and unimportant differences
between the two issues—had *he* done?

A wall-map hung opposite him, showing the extending, polka-
dotted sea, the hanging quadrant of Asia, the huge irregularities
of Australasia, the ruled diagonals of the trade-routes.

He had brought the armoured cruisers of his squadron along
and across some of those trade-routes—from one side of the Pacific
to the other—and whilst doing so and under war conditions, he
had made correct and well-timed rendezvous with his light
cruisers. That the *Dresden* had now come under his command
after her escapades in the Atlantic may have been purely for-
tuitous, but *Nürnberg* and *Leipzig* had rejoined him after voyages
of up to ten thousand miles and this was undeniably a triumph for
an organization which had been under his command and direction
since 1912. Detractors in Berlin would do well to bear that in mind.

Of course, if his judgement of his personal situation were correct, this was a point which his critics would ignore. They would
merely point to the more newsworthy and spectacular exploits of
Emden in the Indian Ocean and suggest that, with ten times the
power, the remaining ships of the East Asiatic Squadron were
hardly to be congratulated upon the fact that they had not sunk
even five times the amount of merchant shipping.

But ten times the power demanded ten times the coal, and
Emden's captain—von Müller—had been extremely lucky with his
fuel problem, catching colliers and provision ships not only at the
right places, but also at the right times. What one small light
cruiser could do among the tangled trade-lanes of the Indian
Ocean bore no relationship whatsoever to the possibilities open to
a whole squadron, or even to one heavy *armoured* cruiser. *Scharnhorst* or *Gneisenau* might well have been drifting helplessly now,
bunkers empty and boilers cold, had he allowed von Schultze or
Maerker to take their ships off on independent operations.

He left the map and walked back to his desk. From a file
he produced a thick, official document which bore his own signature at the bottom, and was headed: 'New Regulations for the

Mobilization of the Cruiser Squadron'. On the first page he found what he was seeking.

> *The probable attitude of the enemy.* The enemy will endeavour to destroy or to hold German warships and to cut off coal supplies by both force and by the exercise of political and business influence on neutral countries. As long as the cruiser squadron continues as such, the enemy will not be able to sub-divide his forces into groups inferior to the cruiser squadron.

He had written that during the previous spring and copies had gone home to the Naval Staff. If they had disagreed with his fundamental premise that a 'Fleet in Being' was of more menace to the enemy than single ships distributed over a wide area, then Berlin should have replaced him immediately. And later on in the Regulations he had made it quite clear that in the event of Japan declaring war on Germany, he would take his command to the west coast of either North or South America where, if Japanese warships attempted to follow, local sympathy and help would immediately swing in his own favour.

As he put the 'New Regulations' back, he found another communication which he had sent to the Naval Staff:

If necessity forces us to give up our plans for attacking commerce, the central position of the South Seas and its numerous hiding-places make it eminently suitable as a base in which to prepare for further operations. No strong enemy forces have bases in the South Seas, or on the west coast of Central or South America. . . . A compact continent, composed of neutral states, offers good facilities for obtaining coal and direct communication with Germany via the auxiliary bases, and there is more traffic off the west coast of South America than in the South Seas, where it will be easier to retain initiative. The delay in the South Seas before proceeding to the west coast, however, will keep the enemy in uncertainty for some time regarding the cruiser squadron's plans. He will consequently be obliged to prepare countermeasures in various areas, thus dissipating his forces.

58

Which was exactly what had happened.

He put away the papers with some relief. There was the answer to any attacks which might be levelled at him from home; there was the answer to certain officers aboard his ships who, reading the reports of von Müller's activities, thought that they should be allowed the chance to win for their own ships the glory which was now—possibly quite deservedly—the *Emden*'s.

And what, after all, had the *Emden* accomplished?

According to the latest information, she had captured eighteen enemy ships, shelled and set fire to oil tanks at Madras, steamed into Penang Harbour and sunk one Russian and one French warship.

She might well do more.

On the other hand she might not. She might be caught herself, and sunk.

There were other events to be considered, however, in any argument for the single raider as against his own scheme for a 'Fleet in Being'—the captures made by *Dresden* and *Leipzig* during the weeks before they had actually joined his flag. *Dresden* had sunk the English steamers *Hyades* and *Holmwood* in the Atlantic, while *Leipzig* had achieved the same success off the coasts of Mexico and Ecuador, capturing and sinking there the steamers *Elsinore* and *Bankfields* respectively.

Such were the facts against him.

And now, to set against this score, for the comparative achievements of those armoured ships which had steamed all the time under his flag.

As upon this comparison must rest his present reputation and possible future, it would be as well to take nothing for granted, to consider it slowly and carefully—best perhaps to ponder the various episodes in proper sequence.

First in order then, would come the descent upon Samoa, shortly after it had passed into Allied hands. An unsatisfactory affair, but one in which he was fully justified in claiming dire misfortune. With any luck at all he should have surprised several steamers in the bay engaged in bringing up provisions for the New

Zealanders who had just occupied the place. With good luck the battle-cruiser *Australia* would have been there as well, and his well-planned torpedo attack upon her might have changed the whole strategic situation in the Southern Hemisphere. But the anchorage had been empty, and as he had not possessed the force necessary to re-take and hold the island—even had it been tactically desirable—he had steamed away without firing a shot, rightly conserving ammunition and sparing native lives.

And from there he had gone to the French possessions at Tahiti, where on 22 September he had sunk a French gunboat in Papeete harbour, silenced the coastal battery and set fire to the copra store —not exactly a resounding victory. It had indeed been somewhat Pyrrhic, for he had failed to obtain there the coal and provisions which he had needed—an original reason for the attack upon the place, more important than the destruction inflicted.

After Papeete, he had first taken his ships to the Marquesas and then on towards Easter Island—and it was on this stage of the long voyage that wireless contact with *Dresden* was first made, and the news obtained that Cradock was coming around the Horn with a squadron of warships. That had been the day upon which his heart beat strong again and he had felt the pride and glory of his profession. Here at last was the real stuff of war for which he had spent his life in ardent preparation : commerce raiding was all right for amateurs, but professional naval seamen fought against professional naval seamen in line of battle.

He and his Chief of Staff, Captain Fielitz, had drawn up plans for action if the English squadron were to reach Easter Island first, and a new purpose and intent had enlivened the deliberations in the wardroom over the after-dinner cigars. When the island had first been sighted as a smudge on the horizon, excitement had gripped all those around him on the flagship's bridge, and binoculars remained glued beneath cap-visors for minutes on end.

But the seas around Easter Island had been empty, and so also the horizons viewed from the top of the black rock which had formed the next point of call in their Odyssey—Más-a-Fuera in the Juan Fernandez group, four hundred and fifty miles from the Chilean coast. So yet more days had passed and more coal burned without adding anything except mileage to the record of the East Asiatic Squadron. By now nearly three months had gone by since the declaration of war, and he would concede that during that time the enemy had suffered little more than inconvenience at his hands.

Until yesterday. Yesterday had changed everything : yesterday was the watershed. In more ways than one, he had now passed the point of no return.

In some respects, that of the naval officer was a damnable profession. Von Spee could so easily have missed Cradock then—as Nelson had missed Napoleon off Crete and later Villaneuve in the West Indies.

If word had not reached von Spee of the *Glasgow*'s presence at Coronel when it did, he would not have searched for the lone cruiser, and the quite inevitable meeting with Cradock might not have taken place until the British squadron had been joined by this Queen class battleship which the agency at Punta Arenas had reported. The search for the *Glasgow* therefore, had discovered the perfect quarry—large enough to cause a battle, but far too weak for any hope of victory—and there was all life's irony in the factors which had probably caused Cradock's movements, too.

Before leaving the last anchorage at Más-a-Fuera for the Chilean coast, von Spee had issued orders that only the auxiliaries were to show themselves above the horizon and that the warships were to remain out of sight of the coast. Moreover, all wireless communications between the ships were to be preceded by the *Leipzig*'s call-sign—as that ship's presence on the coast was known, whilst he sincerely hoped that that of his other ships was not.

It thus seemed highly likely that Cradock's wireless-telegraphists had reported the presence of only one German light cruiser, and while he himself had been moving south after *Glasgow*, Cradock had been moving north after *Leipzig*. Thus had the two squadrons met. Which would, of course, explain why this Queen class battleship, whoever she may be, was not in company.

What a thoroughly hazardous and chancy profession his was!
. . . Cradock, too, had been a member of that profession.

Once on deck, the prospect pleased, the spirits rose. Beneath a
high opalescent sky the ships of his command ploughed serenely
through a light, unangry sea, while to starboard the Chilean coast
showed a dark-blue, scalloped strip. Otherwise the world was his.

From the bridge of *Scharnhorst* he surveyed his fleet, his mind
busy again—but now with the tangible, more tractable problems
of command. His flagship was whole and intact beneath him, her
crew content, her pride assured. Astern came *Gneisenau*, the
flagship's identical yet complementary twin.

His citadels of power.

Alongside, the light cruisers danced in less portentous style.
Leipzig as gallant as a terrier, highly—even brilliantly—efficient;
then *Dresden*, tired perhaps and with a tendency to show it after
her long and arduous commission. Then *Nürnberg*.

There was the weak spot, undoubtedly. It was a great pity that
Nürnberg's boilers were not as sound as her heart—which taken
all in all, must be about the same size. She had spent a week in
dock at San Francisco during July, and if that infernal Serbian had
not so impudently shot the Archduke Ferdinand last June, then
Nürnberg would now be undergoing a thorough and belated overhaul at Tsingtao. ('Der Tag' could undoubtedly have been chosen
with a little more consideration for the outlying squadrons.)
However, a miracle of engineering and a stoic endurance had kept
Nürnberg going, but when she had broken the blades of her port
propeller last month whilst coaling in open roads, the Admiral
really thought that her end had come and that he was to be reduced once again to two scouting cruisers. But her Captain—von
Schönberg—had managed to make good the damage—and if *Nürnberg* could not steam at more than sixteen knots without shaking
herself apart, then that must be the squadron speed. By now her
boilers must be in such a state that it would be dangerous to
exceed that speed anyway.

Von Schönberg was a fine officer and *Nürnberg* a happy ship.

They deserved a reward. Tomorrow they should accompany *Scharnhorst* and *Gneisenau* into Valparaiso, while *Dresden* and *Leipzig* rounded up and guarded the colliers. Their turn would come later.

An excellent idea that, concluded von Spee, for an Admiral should be allowed some little humanity, and his son Otto could come across from *Nürnberg* to visit him and young Heinrich from *Gneisenau*. It would be very pleasant and very refreshing.

His mind came back to his ships. Here were his warships and he had every reason to be extremely proud of them; but where were the others—those essential but sometimes maddeningly obtrusive auxiliaries which accompanied his squadron like wives about a native warrior? He cast his mind back to the orders he had issued on leaving Más-a-Fuera for the Chilean coast four days before. As always, his instructions had been detailed and exact.

1. I intend to get the collier *Santa Isabel* out of Valparaiso.
2. When she has joined up, *Prinz Eitel Friedrich* and *Göttingen* will be despatched to Valparaiso. For this purpose the light cruisers will proceed at twelve knots for Valparaiso and on signal, form scouting line in star formation with *Leipzig* eight miles to port, *Dresden* eight miles to starboard of *Nürnberg*. The cruisers and auxiliaries will remain stopped thirty miles from shore. On *Nürnberg* reporting no enemy in sight, *Prinz Eitel Friedrich* and *Göttingen* will proceed. When they are in safe distance from the harbour, *Nürnberg* is to lead the light cruisers back to the main body.
3. I then intend to proceed along the coast, in line abreast, to Port Low in Guaitecas Island.
4. On the signal 'detach', *Titania* is to proceed to first rendezvous and await there, consuming as little coal as possible, to meet *San Sacramento* and take her to the second rendezvous, where further orders will await her.

Well—a battle had been fought since those orders had been issued and there were changes to be made in addition to those already in hand. *Titania*, for instance, that graceful, delightful but fundamentally useless little tender, had with truly feminine

63

inconsequence captured a sailing vessel on her way to the first rendezvous. She had nearly lost her again almost immediately due to a sudden squall sweeping the *Helicon* away, at far more than eight knots which was about all poor *Titania* could manage these days, but fortunately the prize crew was already on board and managed to hold the Norwegian sailors who manned the *Helicon*. Now her cargo of two thousand six hundred tons of Cardiff coal was safely under way for Más-a-Fuera, and the squadron's bunkers.

But that meant of course, that there was no one to meet *Sacramento*. *Dresden* must go in *Titania*'s place and she and *Leipzig* must round up colliers and send or escort them back to Más-a-Fuera as well. *Baden* should be found easily enough, and perhaps even *Amasis* : doubtless other arrangements could be made for coaling and provisioning whilst at Valparaiso.

Valparaiso. There were other, more crucial matters, to be looked into at Valparaiso, besides those of supply. Where was von Knorr? If by any chance that brilliant, ingenious and highly-reliable ex-Naval Attaché to the Tokyo Embassy were in the neighbourhood, then many of von Spee's more vital problems would be considerably eased, if not solved. If however, Commander von Knorr was not present, then the fate of the East Asiatic Squadron might have to depend upon intelligence reports drafted by consuls, diplomats or other civilian—at any rate non-naval—personnel.

Which was not a prospect the Commander-in-Chief relished.

The squadron steamed north, flags fluttered from the signal halliards, the watches changed, night came.

The Admiral retired early to his night cabin, for he must be fresh and alert tomorrow.

At Valparaiso, 3 *November*

We arrived at Valparaiso this morning. Our Minister Herr Erckerdt soon came aboard, also the Consul-General Gumprecht. The news of our victory had not yet reached here, but spread very quickly. When I landed to call on the local Admirals, there were crowds at the landing places. Cameras clicked everywhere and here and there small groups raised cheers. The Germans of course wanted to celebrate but I positively refused. I was forced however, to spend one and a half hours at their club. On my way back to the boat a lady presented me with a bouquet of flowers.

The day had started badly with the news that although von Knorr was in South America, he was not at Valparaiso. For a short time after the courtesy calls had been paid and during the conferences at the German Consulate, things had improved, for von Spee had been dealing with matters of fact and organization, all of which had gone remarkably well. If von Knorr had not been actually present, there were at any rate signs of his efficiency everywhere, which had been an immense relief. For the first time since leaving Truk in the Carolines, von Spee felt that he was in a position in which his communication and intelligence services were sufficient and intact, and he had been gratified to learn that from Mollendo in the north, to Corral—south of Coronel—German steamers fitted with W/T awaited his bidding. They could slip out at night in order to repeat his signals or to contact him, and for information up and down the length of the Chilean coastline the telephone service and a table of code-words were at his disposal. The system's efficiency had already been proved, for it had been a telephone message from a German ship in Coronel reaching him via the *Göttingen's* radio, which had sent him down after the *Glasgow*—and what had been done successfully once, could equally as successfully be repeated.

Coal supplies too, were for the moment assured. How long the condition would last depended upon a number of circumstances —many beyond his control—but colliers for the next few days could move, and it was up to him to see that they moved to the right places and were not molested on the way. His ability to do this had been confirmed, for inquiries had revealed that instead of a battleship of the Queen class, it had only been the old *Canopus* upon whom Cradock may or may not have been able to fall back : a natural mistake for the agent at Punta Arenas to have made, for the two classes of ships were very similar except in one essential respect—age. *Canopus* had been completed in 1899, the Queens five years later, and the two thousand extra tons which the Queens carried were in armour and engines. If one of *those* had come around the Horn when *Canopus* made the passage, then the battle at Coronel might indeed have been decided differently.

So at the Consulate, all had been well. Von Spee had despatched his report of the action to Naval Staff in Berlin and had received a telegram from them, which although on the surface did not appear to contain good news, was nevertheless a definite confirmation that his ideas were proving correct and finding favour. The telegram read :

Lines of rendezvous in Atlantic are all compromised, all trade routes being strongly patrolled. In the Atlantic cruiser warfare can only be carried on by ships operating in groups. *Karlsruhe* and *Kronprinz Wilhelm* have orders to combine. It is intended to concentrate all forces and order them to break through for home in groups.

Certainly a blow for the 'lone raider' school of thought and justification of his own ineradicable conviction that the proper duty of Naval Forces is to fight Naval Forces—not to fire blank cartridges at unarmed tramps. Whether there was anything in the idea of an attempt to 'break through for home' was an entirely different question. Personally he entertained grave doubts as to its feasibility; a most desirable and tempting project of course, but in view of the enemy fleets massed about the approaches to home waters, holding about as much chance of success as . . . as Cradock had had at Coronel.

Poor Cradock.

A fine man. A seaman and a Naval Officer.

And it was with this sentiment still within the immediate compass of his thoughts that he had yielded to Gumprecht's pressure and called in at the German club, where some drunken, mindless idiot had eventually staggered to his feet, hammered on the table until he had secured the attention of all present, and then invited him—von Spee—to join them all in a toast.

Grinning around him in an insensate triumph which had made von Spee's gorge rise just to watch, the German, the *civilian*, had raised his glass and suggested: 'Damnation to the British Navy!'

That the oaf was not alone in his brutishness was soon apparent too, for the sound of others now lurching to their feet came to von Spee's ears. But as he sat unmoving—welded into his chair by a mixture of horror and unspeakable fury—the hubbub and chatter stilled.

Pushing back his seat, he rose to his full height, glared down the table at the author of the iniquitous proposal, then deliberately picked up his own glass.

'I drink to the memory of a gallant and honourable foe' he announced, and without waiting for support or even compliance drained the glass, threw it on one side, picked up his cocked hat and made for the door—brushing aside the awed and silenced civilians.

Outside, walking down through the sunlit streets, he had recovered something of his composure, and when on the quayside, a woman had stepped forward and presented him with a bouquet, he had been able to accept it with ease and dignity. But it was nevertheless something of a shock to see that the bouquet was one of arum lilies.

He thanked her, adding 'They will do very nicely for my grave.'

And he had brought them on board with him.

But he did not go ashore again, preferring even the scream and rattle of *Scharnhorst*'s winches hoisting in provisions, to the light, unfeeling gossip of uninstructed minds.

CHAPTER SIX

Scharnhorst, *Gneisenau* and *Nürnberg* arrived back at the towering island of Más-a-Fuera, in the Fernandez group, on the afternoon of 6 November, to find *Leipzig* awaiting them there with the collier *Amasis* and the French four-masted barque *Valentine*, captured by *Leipzig* with her cargo of 3,600 tons of Cardiff coal on the afternoon of 3 November. Shortly after the arrival of the armoured cruisers, the collier *Baden* steamed in towing the Norwegian sailing-vessel *Helicon*, with the wayward *Titania* bringing up a triumphant but somewhat lagging rear. *Prinz Eitel Friedrich*—ordered into Valparaiso to provision as soon as the armoured cruisers had left—was due to arrive on 9 November escorting the collier *Santa Isabel*, and on the same day *Dresden* would shepherd in the large collier *San Sacramento*. It appeared to the men of the East Asiatic Squadron that for the moment there was to be no shortage of either coal or provisions.

There was also a welcome addition to the means of transhipping stores and coal into the flats and bunkers of the warships, for some hundreds of seamen and stokers from the German merchantmen in Valparaiso Harbour had offered themselves for enrolment into the Imperial Service, of whom one hundred and twenty-seven had been accepted. An apparently trivial but really crucial problem had also been solved by the capture of the French four-master—that of coalsacks—and her canvas sails were now distributed among the squadron for their once spreading beauty to serve a more menial but vital task.

Coaling was not easy at Más-a-Fuera. It was never a pleasant nor easy task in the best of circumstances, and coaling ships in open roads with a long swell rolling obliquely under the hulls was slow, arduous and dangerous. *Gneisenau* at one time had both *Valentine* and *Helicon* secured alongside, and as the yards of neither sailing-ship had been struck, there was an ever-present danger of pierced funnels or fouled stays and aerials. As the cargoes came inboard, the emptied vessels rode higher and higher out of the water, swinging crazily as their ballast lightened.

But the work kept the crews busy and thus content. The spirit of victory remained with them and the ships were happy.

As far as the officers were concerned, they too moved in an atmosphere of achievement unsullied as yet by doubt. At a conference of senior officers the suggestion was again made that the light cruisers should be allowed more scope for independent operations—the quite reasonable argument being pressed upon the Admiral that the black, voluminous smoke of the armoured cruisers betrayed the squadrons' presence to possible prizes before they were themselves sighted. But von Spee now had a victory with which to bolster his authority and his firm rejection of the proposal was received without rancour. When on 10 November—three days after the conference—it was learned that *Emden* had at last been caught and sunk, all ideas for operations involving single ships evaporated.

The idea of a break-through for home too, despite the fundamental doubts as to its possibility in more thoughtful minds, was a tempting dream which acted as a common hope to unify the squadron. It was certainly a long way back home to the Fatherland, but then they had already come a long way—and in the prevailing atmosphere of confidence all things seemed possible. As Berlin had proposed the scheme, presumably the High Seas Fleet would be ordered out to co-operate during the final approach through the enemy-controlled seas. Certainly the Naval Staff seemed most anxious to help, repeating their suggestions for combined action with other raiders in the Atlantic, pressing von Spee for details regarding his coal and provision requirements, giving him particulars of existing and proposed German wireless stations which would aid him during the voyage. They also filled in the picture of the general situation which now existed in southern waters as a result of the Coronel victory.

Over one hundred thousand tons of British mercantile shipping had been brought virtually to a standstill along the western seaboard of South America and on the eastern coast as far north as the Plate. Shipments of tin, copper and copper ore were sealed in harbour, the export of alpaca wool from Peru and of saltpetre from Chile were stopped—indeed at one time during that month it looked as though this vital Chilean industry would be brought to a complete standstill through the lack of trade. It was unfortunate that Germany could not buy this essential war material, but Britain blocked the northern end of the trade route just as von Spee controlled the southern, and the neutral countries in between just had to accept the economic strain. In all, ninety-one out of one hundred and thirty-four factories along the Chilean coast were obliged to close down. The results were not immediately apparent, but by the end of November the German cause was not so popular as it had been at the beginning.

The main problem facing von Spee, of course, would always be the same one which beset his antagonist, by now about to hoist his flag at Devonport—the whereabouts of the enemy forces. At this time the German Admiral had little immediate worry and his Intelligence was secure enough for him to know it. H.M.S. *Glasgow* was apparently licking her wounds either in Montevideo or at the Falklands and although the whereabouts of *Canopus* and *Otranto* had not yet been established, they were not strong enough either separately or together to constitute a menace.

The fate of *Good Hope*, too, was now established beyond all doubt. Not only had the British Admiralty tacitly admitted her loss by failing categorically to deny it, but shortly after the *Leipzig*'s arrival at Más-a-Fuera, Captain Haun was told by some of his men that about ten minutes after the squadron had formed line abreast to sweep across the battle-area in search of the vanished enemy, the ship had steamed through a mass of debris. To those on the bridge searching the darkness ahead for signs of movement or a renewal of action, this had not been apparent, but the men on the lower deck engaged in throwing empty ammunition-cases overboard had seen floating spars and chests, a waterlogged upturned boat, and drifting hammocks, some with men still draped across them. There had been no sign of life, no call for help: the seas were high and the enemy still at hand, so no attempt could have been made to investigate further.

When told of this, Admiral von Spee preserved an immobile silence—then broke it to ask brusquely after the state of the ammunition lockers and of the coaling. The vital day-to-day business of the squadron occupied all minds and acted as anodyne to those whose clarity disturbed their owners.

As far as the ammunition supplies were concerned, an obvious course had been taken and it was redistributed to equalize the magazines. In reply to one of the Naval Staff inquiries von Spee was eventually able to answer that each armoured cruiser carried four hundred and forty-five rounds of heavy ammunition and eleven hundred rounds of secondary, while the light cruisers carried eighteen hundred and sixty rounds of 4.1-inch apiece. This was not an entirely satisfactory situation. During the recent action *Scharnhorst* had fired off four hundred and twenty-two rounds of 8.2-inch, of which two hundred and thirty-four had been armour-piercing and the rest high explosive. Another Coronel would leave her defenceless—a problem which only the Naval Staff could solve. Perhaps they were already engaged in doing so.

As far as fuel was concerned, for the moment it was only the never-ending task of transferring it from ship to ship which presented the difficulties. An officer aboard *Gneisenau* made the following entries in his diary during the stay at Más-a-Fuera :

6 November. Arrived p.m. *Leipzig* coaling from *Helicon*.
7 November. Coaling from two sailing-ships.
8 November. Coaling from *Valentine*.
9 November. Our coaling finished. *Sacramento* with *Dresden*

arrived. *Prinz Eitel Friedrich* arrived. Took in 1,440 tons provisions.

10 November.   *Sacramento* transferred to first division. *Leipzig* left for Valparaiso at midday.

11 November.   Weather moderated. At ten o'clock hands sent on board *Valentine*.

12 November.   Transferred coal from *Valentine* to *Baden*.

13 November.   Still coaling.

14 November.   Coaling *Amasis* from *Sacramento*.

15 November.   Coaling *Baden* and *Amasis* from *Sacramento*.

It was wearying and monotonous work, but by the time they were ready to leave Más-a-Fuera, each armoured cruiser was laden with bunkers filled to their 2,000-ton capacity, while the light cruisers had coal heaped on the decks to raise their capacity to a thousand tons. In addition, they were accompanied by the large colliers *Amasis* and *Baden* both with full cargoes. The Norwegian sailing-vessel *Helicon* had to be released, as only her cargo was enemy property.

On the afternoon of 16 November (as Sturdee was approaching St Vincent on the first leg of his journey south), the ships of the East Asiatic Squadron quitted Más-a-Fuera and steamed south.

Among factors which contributed to this move was the receipt of information that heavy units of the Japanese Fleet were in movement to the northwards—somewhere in the region of the Galapagos Islands—but it is not inconceivable that by this time Graf von Spee himself had been brought to a frame of mind when he was half-persuaded that he would one day lead his ships back to a victorious welcome in the Fatherland.

By now he had received three telegrams from Berlin, all urging him to undertake this seemingly impossible feat, and in reply to the last one he sent off a message just before the squadron sailed, stating categorically : 'The cruiser squadron intends to break through for home.'

It is a little difficult to believe that so shrewd a man and so competent a sailor would allow himself the luxury of wishful thinking, but it seems likely that in the atmosphere of triumph which still pervaded the squadron, his mistrust of the confidence and elation of the communications from Berlin began to evaporate. Certainly the Naval Staff telegrams were most encouraging, urging him to issue orders to German agencies along the route for the supplies which he would need, in terms which suggested that those supplies would be instantly forthcoming.

He knew by now—and beyond reasonable doubt—that he had nothing to fear either from enemy action or lack of supplies in the area stretching south from his present position to the Horn. His talks in the Consulate at Valparaiso together with the reports which had reached him at Más-a-Fuera had assured him of that.

What awaited him around the Horn?

Incredibly—nothing!

As far as his Intelligence organization could discover, the Allies had still made no attempt to fill the inexplicable power-vacuum between Tierra del Fuego and the Plate, and if he could round the Horn while this state of affairs continued then there was no reason why his squadron should not reach Gill Bay—an anchorage some eight hundred miles north of the Horn on the Patagonian coastline, which *Dresden* had already once used for coaling.

With this in mind, on 18 November he issued the following orders to the agencies at La Plata and New York:

Send steamers—German if possible—to arrive at Port Santa Elena on 5 December, with 10,000 tons coal and provisions for 1,000 men for three months. No oil. Intelligence reports particularly desirable.

Once there, unscathed and unmolested, he could coal and provision at greater speed and in much more comfortable conditions than at Más-a-Fuera—and with bunkers full could face the gauntlet of the North Atlantic with some degree of confidence. To give something more than moral support to that confidence, he followed his instructions to the agencies with the following fiat to Berlin:

New York and La Plata are to arrange for the dispatch of 20,000 tons

of coal, 5,000 awaiting orders at Pernambuco on 1 January, 15,000 at New York from 20 January.
Also at New York provisions for 2,000 men for three months.

The arrangement of supplies on such a scale and under such conditions would be a mark of good faith on the part of the Naval Staff, and if they carried them out it would be unlikely that they would then fail to co-operate to the full on that last, most dangerous stage around the enemy's flank and down through the North Sea. If by chance or enemy design the agencies on the western Atlantic seaboard could not fulfil the demands, then possibly the German possessions in Togoland and the Cameroons were still in a position to help—although there had been rumours in Valparaiso that all African Territories were being closely invested by the British.

But then there had also been rumours that the British had a rebellion on their hands in South Africa.

Which was true? Either—or even both?

This lack of information on the overall strategic position was frustrating. He would have to wait now in whatever patience he could muster until *Dresden* and *Leipzig* rejoined after their trip to show the flag once again in Valparaiso. The second Naval Staff Officer, Commander von Botticher, had accompanied the *Dresden* in order to gather what news he could, and until then there was nothing further a Commander-in-Chief could do.

Except to plot, and plan, and try to cover every eventuality.

And that he had already done—a thousand times.

As the squadron steamed south, the weather worsened, the thermometer fell, and the prospect of fog and rain which lay immediately ahead was productive of gloominess of spirit in men used to cruising in the tropics. There had also been one or two events of late which might be said to have planted the seeds of melancholy throughout the squadron.

First there had been the news of the fall of their naval base of Tsingtao on 7 November—inevitable of course, but not less sad-

74

dening because of it. They had all spent many happy months on the East Asiatic Station and their pleasure had been increased by the pride which any German could rightly take in the town and the colony which surrounded it. It had been a model of German colonial development, and the thought that it was now in Japanese hands was disquieting, especially for those attached by bonds of romance or kinship to its valiant inhabitants.

The other two events which had contributed greatly to depression had been of less importance, but to sailors of feeling, much greater impact. The French sailing-ship *Valentine* had been a beautiful ship, practically new and a superb example of the ship-builder's craft. Steel hull, masts and yards had given her a slenderness and grace even in excess of that of the old-time clippers, and it had been with genuine sorrow that her destruction had been both ordered by the Admiral and carried out by the men. She had been stripped of everything which could possibly be of use to the squadron, but the higher she rode out of the water and the barer her hull and upperworks became, the more simple and graceful had her lines appeared. In the end she had slid beneath the waves like a dying bird in a poem by Heine, and those who watched had also mourned.

And if the end of the *Valentine* had touched them all, that of *Titania* had left a hollow beneath their hearts. She had come across the Pacific with them, her outworn engines giving her an inconsequence of behaviour which made everyone laugh while they cursed her. But what had been a matter of rueful amusement in the comparative safety of the wide Pacific could be a fatal weakness in narrower, enemy-patrolled waters. Moreover Cape Horn weather would certainly prove too much for *Titania*'s boilers—so sadly, her destruction had been ordered and carried out. She had won all their hearts, and she had always provided a lucky few with a haven of rest, calm and refreshment during the periods when the cruisers were in the unendurable chaos of coaling. When at last she had lain over on her side in the shadow of the great rock, it had been a moment of poignant grief.

The seas were barren when they closed above her.

The waves rose, the rain lanced across the decks, the wind howled threateningly.

At noon on 21 November, the squadron steamed through fog and sleet into San Quentin Sound on the north side of Penas Gulf, and anchored beneath a glacier which fell to the water's edge in smooth folds like a lady's cape. The anchorage was undeniably in Chilean waters and the squadron had no right to be there, but the Allies had used Vallenar Bay nearby with impunity, and, as it happened, other evidence came soon to light that the British had used (and doubtless were still using) other illegal coaling places in neutral waters. *Dresden* captured the English steamer *North Wales* on 18 November whilst coming south from Valparaiso, and her log-book revealed that Cradock had coaled his ships in Corcovado Bay.

Not that it mattered. Civilian-made neutrality laws were rightly disregarded by practical seamen, who coaled where they could, knew that others did likewise, and treated the shrill plaints of politicians and journalists with the contempt which they deserved.

Here the water was still, deep and dark—and on it floated the auxiliaries *Seydlitz*, *Memphis* and *Ramses*. More ships would arrive with more fuel and stores—and, it was to be hoped, more intelligence reports.

There was work for all again.

The collier *Seydlitz* had left Valparaiso on 20 October, with 4,150 tons of coal and an ample supply of water and provisions, but she could obviously not have brought with her any later news than that which had been available to von Spee at the same place in November. *Memphis*, however, had come around from Punta Arenas (bringing 2,400 tons) and as she had only left that port on 19 November, she should be the bearer of late—and possibly reliable—intelligence.

She was—but having listened to it, it appears that von Spee was disinclined to believe it.

On 15 November, reported Captain Ebeling, a British steamer had put into Punta Arenas after having called at the Falkland Islands, where she had been unable to discharge her cargo owing to the fact that the place was practically abandoned. The warships which had been at Port Stanley—according to members of the steamer's crew—had been ordered away at full speed for the Cape of Good Hope to put down an insurrection there which threatened British interests in the southern part of the African continent. As a result, at least up as far as the Plate and possibly right up to Pernambuco, British shipping was unprotected.

As indeed, the intelligence reports had seemed to suggest.

It must have taken von Spee a decided effort of will to resist the temptation to believe these reports, for the opportunities they seemed to offer him to take advantage of gaps in the enemy's defences were alluring. This information regarding troubles for the British in South Africa had by now reached him from two entirely separate and distinct sources, and as an explanation of that power-vacuum between the Horn and the Plate, it was most plausible. Possibly it was so plausible as to seem to von Spee positively specious, for although he was well aware (none more so) of the immense problems involved in moving large and powerful warships across the wide seas, he was also aware of the long columns of close print which made up the lists of ships of the Royal Navy. Perhaps he considered that problems of space and time should be capable of solution in this case by sheer weight of numbers.

At the back of von Spee's mind remained always the thought that Britain had, over the years, built up a vast, world-embracing empire despite the fact that she was herself a tiny and almost insignificant island. She could not have done this without combining intelligence of a very high order with other qualities of enterprise and determination—and the fact that of late years von Spee, in common with all other General or Flag Officers in the Imperial Service, had been encouraged to view this proposition in rather different terms, really made no difference to its ultimate conclusion. Call her intelligence low cunning if you wish (or if the Naval Staff wish), and her enterprise and determination respectively piracy and ruthless exploitation—in the end it still left Great Britain a power to be reckoned with.

She had not incorporated that qualitative adjective into her name without possessing at least the ability to lay a trap for the unwary, just as well as any other world power and possibly better than most. Her rulers had had long experience of imperial government and the conduct of war—and in naval warfare she possessed greater experience than the rest of the world put together. It was all very well for politicians and administrators suddenly to state that Great Britain was an empty power and the Royal Navy a spent and out-of-date force, but they had not passed their formative years in an institution which regarded that force in much the light of a respected and model elder brother.

Grand Admiral von Tirpitz himself had regarded Plymouth as for all intents and purposes his own home port during his cadetship, and von Spee had risen through the junior naval ranks with the efficiency and integrity of the Royal Navy deliberately and continuously held out to him as an ideal for which the Imperial Navy must ever strive. He sympathized deeply with his own junior officers, who had been thunderstruck when the news had arrived that Great Britain was an enemy. Senior officers, conditioned to a certain extent by the confidential memoranda issued from Berlin, had not been so astonished—but there existed among them nevertheless a curious dichotomy of thought as a result of their attempts to reconcile an ingrained admiration for the Royal Navy, with a suddenly expedient dislike and disdain. Some managed it, but not all—and von Spee lacked the chameleon instinct. He could not forget his own training; neither could he forget the picture of naval perfection and efficiency which the sight of the White Ensign had always conjured up in his mind, nor the memory of the tradition which held that whatever else might happen beforehand, the last battle was always won by Great Britain.

If the Falkland Islands were apparently unguarded, it might well be because they were being held out to him as a bait—and even if they weren't, it seems that in those early days in San Quentin Sound, von Spee did not consider their capture and occupation important enough to tempt him from his homeward course. After all, such a *coup de main* would only present him with more administrative problems, whilst the practical advantages to be obtained from it appeared nebulous, to say the least. He would certainly not have time to make use of the dockyard installations at Port Stanley, much though some of his ships could do with attention and repair, and as for the coal stocks, if the Naval Staff in Berlin were as good as their word and even a quarter as good as their encouragement, then the dumps would not constitute the slightest temptation for him to go there.

Of course, to land a force on a British possession and occupy it, however temporarily, would be an enormous blow to England's prestige—but then so would the arrival of the ships of the East Asiatic Squadron in the Baltic, and that would be a blow infinitely more satisfying to both himself and his men.

No—unless far better reasons arose for their capture than were immediately apparent, the Falkland Islands should not lure him from his homeward journey—either to destruction or even to temporary triumph. As far as he was concerned they could remain undisturbed and inviolate in their chilly and somewhat barren isolation. If his ships and his men were to return to the Fatherland, then he must plan to that end only, and in the meantime there were many matters requiring his attention; for instance, that of present physical conditions. They were not very agreeable.

Coaling was in progress, and now he had no escape from it into the calm and peace which *Titania* had always provided. The winches howled, the huge crane amidships clanked and rattled, coal crashed down into the bunkers, and its insidious, infuriating black mist spread through the ship like a miasma which attacked the spirit and temper instead of the body. He must watch himself or some quite insignificant mishap would rasp his nerves and they would drag him towards that pit of black, consuming anger which always awaited him just beyond the circle of control.

Coal.

Coal—God in heaven—Coal! His mind and memory were full to overflowing with facts and figures concerning the wretched stuff. *Scharnhorst* and *Gneisenau* would each burn two hundred tons every day if they steamed at fifteen knots, and if they raced ahead at twenty knots, then even in good weather their bunkers would be empty in less than five days and two thousand miles. Against a head sea fifteen hundred miles might well be their maximum—and they had a Horn passage ahead of them. The light cruisers could take three thousand tons aboard between them, and with *Dresden*'s turbines in the shape they were, she at least would need re-coaling before Santa Elena.

Between Galapagos Island and the Horn, 35,000 tons had been distributed, and although some of it was still to the north, he would need every ounce if all his ships were to reach home. And more: 15,000 tons at New York; 5,000 tons at Pernambuco; 10,000 tons at Santa Elena. And he must bear in mind the fact that the Royal Navy knew of—and might well be using—the anchorage near Santa Elena at Gill Bay: already he had lost 6,000 tons to the Australian squadron in the Carolines.

While crossing the Pacific the armoured cruisers and their consorts had burned nearly 17,000 tons. The 5,000 tons awaiting them at Más-a-Fuera had gone by the time they reached Valparaiso on the day after the battle: that was the ever-present menace to careful husbanding of supplies—action or a long chase could wreck the calculations of the most prudent quartermaster.

Thank heavens the colliers had been at Penas Gulf: *Seydlitz* with 4,510 tons, *Ramses*, *Memphis* with 2,400 tons, *Amasis*, *Santa Isobel*, *Baden*—but they all *burned* coal too, just as they carried it. So many colliers, so many miles behind them now. The *Elsbeth*, sunk by the *Minotaur*, the *Longmoon*, the *Senegallia*, the *Freesia*, the *Markomannia* who had accompanied the *Emden* and presumably shared her fate; the *Governeur Jashke*, the *Staats Sekretar Kratke*, the O.I.D. *Ahlers*—their names echoed in his mind like a roll of honour.

Where were they all now? Some sunk, some interned in neutral harbours, some still at large—for how long? (The *Amasis* must go south as soon as her holds were empty. He must see Lieutenant zur Helle before she goes.)

What savings could be affected? Could they risk keeping only two dynamos running as they had done in the Pacific? No need now for the refrigeration and ventilating plant, so perhaps that would be possible—but no, the men would need warmth below now, hot pipes instead of fans. Could turret engines and torpedo main air pumps be kept at ten minutes' notice by day? Possibly down as far as the Horn anyway. Better say until off the western entrance to Magellan.

What else could be done?

Little enough. If the coal supplies were at the rendezvous to meet him, the penny-pinching would not be necessary—and if they were not there to meet him then the most rigid economy could not take his ships more than another hundred miles along a journey of eight thousand. But he must watch the speed, and a following sea would make an enormous difference over a long period.

But first of all he must get around the Horn.

With the recent thought still in his memory regarding the possibility of British warships coaling in Gill Bay however, he took the opportunity to amend his instructions to La Plata. A signal went off to Valparaiso for forwarding to the agency, to the effect that the colliers must not be there before the squadron—which would arrive on 5 December.

He was not to know that Valparaiso thankfully annotated this telegram : 'Coal and provisions from Chile therefore no longer under consideration'.

He was outstaying his welcome.

Two days after the arrival of the cruiser squadron in Penas Gulf, the collier *Luxor* arrived from Coronel with 3,600 tons of coal and—far more important—Commander von Knorr aboard. The commander was accompanied by a Dr Schenk, who lost little time in spreading the news that a battle-cruiser of the High Seas Fleet was to break out into the North Atlantic to meet them, bringing provisions, ammunition and secret orders telling of the co-operation and welcome which would be extended to the East Asiatic Squadron upon that last dangerous but surely victorious dash for home. The names of the powerful ships *Moltke*, *Von der Tann* and their best collier's namesake *Seydlitz* were bandied about, with excellent results upon the morale of practically everybody.

The exceptions were Admiral von Spee and his immediate staff, for they were quick to realize that what Schenk was disseminating as hard and fast agreements, had not in fact proceeded any further than suggestions made to the Naval Staff by von Knorr. There was no proof that Berlin had concurred, and von Knorr also brought news which cast doubt upon the likelihood that they ever would, for the terms of their encouragement to von Spee to issue his orders to the American agencies were now seen to have been rather too optimistic. It appeared extremely doubtful if the agencies could execute them all.

For instance, the five thousand tons of coal which von Spee had requested the Naval Staff to arrange at Pernambuco on 1 January would probably be there—but it was unlikely that it would ever leave territorial waters in order to meet him at sea, for neutral countries were suddenly proving unco-operative. Perhaps they had learned from Chile's example and had no wish to close down their major industries, but whatever the reaction among the countries of South America, that in North America was unmistakably hostile. Canada of course was an enemy country anyway, but the agency at New York held out very little hope that either coal or provisions would ever be allowed to leave the coasts of the United States for the East Asiatic Squadron.

On the other hand, full colliers did await von Spee on the other side of the Atlantic in the Canaries. There were four thousand tons at Palma and eight thousand at Teneriffe—and once he had chased away the enemy patrols, the colliers could sail to meet him at any rendezvous he cared to indicate (within reason, of course). All he had to do was to arrive in the area at the end of a five thousand mile journey up from Santa Elena, with sufficient coal in his bunkers to fight an action with whatever warships Britain chose to keep there. As at the outbreak of the war the 5th Cruiser Squadron had been based on Sierra Leone, it was apparently assumed that the worst that could befall von Spee was another Coronel—for the 5th Cruiser Squadron had then consisted of *Carnarvon*, *Cornwall*, *Cumberland* and *Monmouth*, and one at least of those ships was now at the bottom of the sea.

No information was offered to von Spee regarding replacements which Britain might have sent down—in fact there was no up-to-date information whatsoever available as to the extent and distribution of British naval forces in the whole of the Atlantic. One of the reasons for this, as the Admiral knew, was that whereas before Coronel, British W/T had been active and easily recognizable—thus considerably aiding the task of identifying the forces and pinpointing their positions—since the battle it had been virtually non-existent. It was left to him to decide the reasons for this, and also to deduce from his own knowledge and experience what the enemy were up to—bearing in mind all the time, of course, that Britain was an empty power and the Royal Navy a spent force.

As further proof of this was offered the news that the best that England could produce to fill the highest post at the Admiralty was an old, retired sailor, seventy-four years of age and obviously practically in his dotage. Fisher, his name was—Graf von Spee might remember him from the days when as Admiral Sir John Fisher he had commanded the Mediterranean Fleet at the turn of the century.

As it happened, von Spee did remember Fisher, but at the news of his re-appointment, the Vice-Admiral showed curiously little jubilation.

He showed in fact, little except growing impatience in all his dealings with Dr Schenk, pointing out rather brusquely that before he was prepared to waste time and nervous energy on preparations for his reception in the vicinity of the Canaries, he wanted to know what chances he had of ever arriving there. Could the agencies fulfil the demands made in his first telegram, for ten thousand tons and provisions for three months to be sent to Port Santa Elena on the Patagonian coast?

The situation in this regard was that no news should be taken for good news. There seemed to be more trouble in regard to actual shipping than to the coal and stores themselves, and from what the various consulates had indicated (to Dr Schenk) it would seem to be advisable for as many colliers as possible to accompany the cruiser squadron around the Horn. This would now be a necessity in any case in order to cross the Atlantic to the Canaries, but as far as prospective cargoes for the colliers were concerned, there was just as strong a German civilian element in Argentina as there was in Chile—and there was surely no reason to doubt that co-operation with the gallant Admiral would be just as satisfactory, and yield just as fruitful and felicitous results.

With that the Admiral had for the moment to be content, but there was some sugar for the pill whose bitterness was not yet completely apparent.

By order of the Kaiser, Admiral Graf von Spee had been awarded the Iron Cross, First Class, and also the Iron Cross, Second Class—and in addition he was to choose from the officers and men who had served under his flag so brilliantly from Tsingtao to South America, three hundred others to receive the Iron Cross, Second Class. There were also many presents aboard *Luxor* for the heroes of the East Asiatic Squadron—and would the Admiral kindly indicate how they were to be distributed?

Rear-Admiral Sir Christopher Cradock, K.C.V.O., C.B., M.V.O.

H.M.S. *GLASGOW*
Built January 1911: Two 6-inch guns: Ten 4-inch guns.

A.M.C. *OTRANTO*
'. . . for what use a merchantman would be in a naval battle'

H.M.S. *GOOD HOPE*
Built 1902: Two 9.2-inch guns: Sixteen 6-inch guns

H.M.S. *MONMOUTH*
Built 1903:
Fourteen 6-inch guns

H.M.S. *CANOPUS*
'. . . the forlorn hope'
Built 1899:
Four 12-inch guns:
Twelve 6-inch guns

Winston Churchill and Admiral Lord Fisher leaving Whitehall

Sinking the tender *Titania* off Más-a-Fuera, 15 November 1914

Scharnhorst, *Gneisenau* and *Nürnberg* leaving Valparaiso Bay, 4 November 1914. Ships of the Chilean Navy are in the foreground

Vice-Admiral Graf von Spee

S.M.S. *SCHARNHORST*
Built 1907, sister-ship to *Gneisenau*: Eight 8.2-inch guns: Six 6-inch guns

Vice-Admiral Sir Frederick Doveton Sturdee, K.C.B., C.M.G., C.V.O., in Captain's uniform

H.M.S. *INVINCIBLE*
Built 1908: Eight 12-inch guns: Sixteen 4-inch guns

The guns of *Inflexible*

H.M.S. *INFLEXIBLE*
Sister-ship to Invincible. A photograph taken after the removal of the
4-inch guns from the turrets

H.M.S. *BRISTOL*
Sister-ship to Glasgow. At Rio de Janeiro in 1918

H.M.S. *CARNARVON*
Built 1905: Four 7.5-inch guns: Six 6-inch guns
Flagship of Rear-Admiral A. P. Stoddart

H.M.S. *CORNWALL*
Built 1904: Fourteen 6-inch guns

H.M.S. *KENT*
Built 1903, *sister-ship to Cornwall*: Fourteen 6-inch guns

'Enemy approaching Port William, Falkland Isles, 8.12.14.' Lieut-Commander Verner's view from the fore-top of *Inflexible*, as *Canopus* opened fire from Port Stanley

Another water-colour by Lieut-Commander Verner, showing 'last rounds falling about *Scharnhorst* two minutes after silencing her and just before she turned towards *Inflexible*, on fire fore and aft, and obviously sinking'

Survivors from *Gneisenau* after the Battle of the Falkland Islands,
8th December 1914

S.M.S. *DRESDEN*
After her surrender at Más-a-Fuera, with the white flag at the foremast.
Built 1908: Ten 4.1-inch guns

CHAPTER SEVEN

At four o'clock on the afternoon of 26 November, within hours of the arrival at Abrolhos Rocks of *Invincible* and *Inflexible*, the ships of the East Asiatic Squadron steamed west out of Penas Gulf and then south into the teeth of what was to be a memorable storm.

The wind, fresh when they cleared the gulf, rose steadily until by late evening it was a driving fury piling up the sea into rollers as high as a house and with half a mile between them. Blown spray sheeted from the crests and drummed a harsh tattoo on decks and canvas screens, while halliards and stays sang like cello-strings tuning up for a symphony of violence. At first the power and height above water of the armoured cruisers kept them riding over the sea with nothing worse than discomfort, amply compensated by the exhilaration of fighting a gale in a taut ship. But when the short Antarctic night came, it brought no diminution of wind and the sea was rising all the time.

With darkness came loss of contact between the ships : dawn revealed the squadron and their escorts scattered over a grey waste, each ship locked in battle with forces of unbelievable malevolence. The men of the East Asiatic Squadron were certainly learning the full significance of a Horn Passage, and the scene from the bridge of *Gneisenau* became one of shapeless tumult. As her bows rose towards the curling head of the next wave and the ship crawled over its heaving back, the wind would scoop tons of solid water from the crest and hurl it down upon her decks with

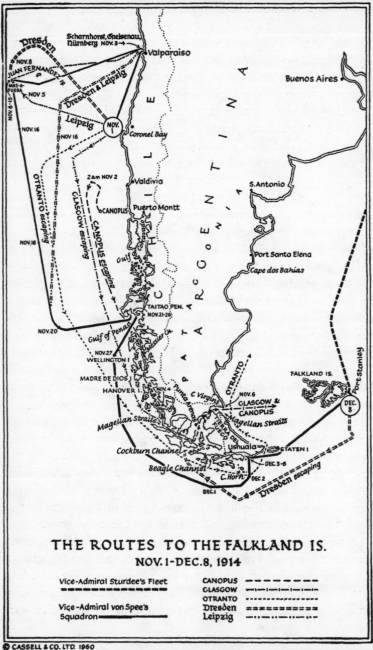

Dresden

NOV. 8

JUAN FERNANDEZ IS.

MAS-A-FUERA

NOV. 5

NOV. 6-15

NOV. 16

Scharnhorst, Gneisenau, Nürnberg NOV. 3-4

Valparaiso

Dresden & Leipzig

Leipzig

NOV. 16

NOV. 1

Coronel Bay

Buenos Aires

OTRANTO escaping

NOV. 18

NOV. 20

2 am NOV 2

Valdivia

GLASGOW escaping

CANOPUS escaping

CANOPUS

Puerto Montt

Gulf of Corcovado

S. Antonio

Port Santa Elena

Cape dos Bahias

C H I L E

A R G E N T I N A

P A T A G O N I A

TAITAO PEN.

NOV. 21-26

Gulf of Penas

NOV. 27

WELLINGTON I.

MADRE DE DIOS

HANOVER I.

Wheeler Ch.

Magellan Straits

Cockburn Channel

Beagle Channel

NOV. 4

Punta Arenas

C. Virgins

TIERRA DEL FUEGO

Ushuaia

C. Horn

DEC. 1

OTRANTO

NOV. 6

GLASGOW & CANOPUS

Magellan Straits

STATEN I.

DEC. 3-6

DEC. 2

Dresden escaping

FALKLAND IS.

Port Stanley

DEC. 8

THE ROUTES TO THE FALKLAND IS.
NOV. 1 - DEC. 8, 1914

Vice-Admiral Sturdee's Fleet

Vice-Admiral von Spee's Squadron

CANOPUS

GLASGOW

OTRANTO

Dresden

Leipzig

© CASSELL & CO. LTD. 1960

the sound of toppling masonry. Green torrents, white-flecked with rage, raced along the waist, then sucked overboard with a reluctant sob as though in torment at their failure to drag the ship down with them. Back over the bows they came again, and then again, wrenching away at the deck fittings, foaming around masts and funnels, reaching for unsecured prey.

Then for a second the triangle of forecastle would be silhouetted hard-edged against the racing clouds, a wave-crest would snarl its way under the hull, the bows drop away and the whole ship plunge down into the trough to bury herself as far as the foremast in sea suddenly as smooth and menacing as molten bottle-glass. As the stern dropped, the waters would lift and break, spooned up by the rising bows until they flooded back along the decks and over the sides in cascades and jets of snow-white irresistibility.

Then the whole process would start again—and as the day wore on, the waves loomed higher and higher like mountain ridges come suddenly to nightmare life. Sometimes the men on the bridge caught brief glimpses of *Scharnhorst*, always wrapped in a cloud of spray and often apparently hull-deep in the tumult. It was impossible to breathe while facing into the screaming wind, and to turn away and watch astern revealed a scene to stop the heart, for there wallowed and pitched the smaller ships of the squadron.

If the armoured cruisers were flooded, the light cruisers were virtually submerged. Heavily-cargoed anyway, the excess coal heaped on their decks made them top-heavy, and their masts and funnels flicked through impossible arcs like frantic signals for help. As the armoured cruisers slowed to allow them to come up and keep company if not formation, the *Nürnberg* was seen labouring gamely out of the troughs until the wind could catch her again and press her down—while the seas, flogged into maniacal frenzy, leaped up along her sides and seemed to close above them.

A wave would fling itself past and away astern, *Nürnberg* would hang for a second with her battered screws spinning high in the air, then drop out of sight like a lorry going over the edge of a cliff. Yet when *Gneisenau* crashed through the wave crest and down into the trough beside her, she would already be moving forward again, creeping up into the welter of spite which awaited her on the shoulder of the next wave.

Conditions aboard the light cruisers were appalling. Hot food or dry clothing was out of the question. Only the stokers were not frozen to the marrow in the increasingly bitter cold—and they worked in constant danger of being thrown against red-hot plates or buried under shifting coal as their ships twisted, rolled, pitched or stood on their heads. Ropeways were rigged throughout the ships and across the decks wherever they had a chance of survival and no one could move without their support—and often on the upper deck not even with it, for the precious coal was giving added destructive power to the raging seas.

Some of the deck cargoes had been struck down as soon as the force of the impending violence had been realized, but not all, and that which had been piled loose was caught by the seas and sent crashing about, a dreadful, treacherous menace under two feet of surging water. Eventually, the blocks broke themselves down into pieces small enough to go out through the scuppers, but not until they had wreaked untold damage in the process. Some of the coal had been stacked in crates and boxes and as these disintegrated under the hammering of the loose coal, more blocks were released to add their weight to the destructive powers. Deck gear was smashed away or worked loose, boats jumped in their chocks and stove themselves in, ventilators were reduced to crumpled sheets of metal and steel ladders torn loose and twisted up like wirework.

And all the time the wind howled and wailed and sobbed and screamed until ears were deafened and senses numbed.

There seemed no end to it. All through the second and third day the storm raged, holding the squadron back from the Horn, keeping their speed down to eight knots as a maximum and often to less than five—yet all the time they burned fuel as though they were steaming at fifteen knots, and a fair fraction of what they didn't burn went overboard. By 29 November, the ships were off the western entrance to Magellan Straits, the deck cargoes had gone and the bunkers were emptying—but at least the light cruisers were riding easier. *Dresden*, who needed most, had also lost most, for her crew had flung thirty tons overboard before the gale reached its full fury.

But what afforded relief to his men must have been a matter of some concern to von Spee. He viewed their passage around the Horn mathematically—so many tons meant so many miles, and he knew only too well that the laws of logistics contain no compassionate elasticity as a reward for endurance. Every block of coal thrown or washed overboard decreased their chances of reaching home—and possibly even of survival, for Dr Schenk's news of shipping difficulties had at last been confirmed by a telegram from Buenos Aires via Valparaiso, which did not, however, also confirm the doctor's confidence in other matters.

It read:

Inform cruiser squadron that coal cannot be sent from Argentine or Brazilian ports, coal exports being prohibited. East coast of South America is *importing* coal from North America only. If the cruiser squadron comes to the east coast it is advisable for it to bring as many colliers as possible in company.

If the telegram was to be taken at its face value, then in conjunction with the news that von Knorr had brought, this meant that between Penas Gulf and the Canaries von Spee must manage with the coal already in the bunkers and holds of his ships now in company, plus any enemy cargoes which might fall into his hands. However, if the Admiral had distrusted the easy optimism of the communications from the Naval Staff, he was now prepared to extend the same sceptical attitude to the pessimism contained in those from the agencies. Doubtless Valparaiso was urging La Plata to greater efforts and doubtless some results would be obtained.

The question was—how great would those results be? Another uncertainty to add to those with which he was already beset! And of course this matter of continual doubt upon practically every important aspect of his problems affected the vital matter of confidence. If Berlin could not fulfil the pledges implicit in their communications, was it likely that when the time came they would risk units of the High Seas Fleet to help him home? Not, of course, that they had ever made concrete promises on that or indeed any other subject—but they had undoubtedly advised him to make for home waters, and in doing so had assured him of help in matters of coal and provisions at least.

It now appeared that to the extent that this last telegram was true, those assurances of help were empty—but he had no means of gauging the proportion of truth or emptiness. If the telegram were completely true and there was no help at all forthcoming, then he and his command were heading for a fatal impasse, and it was extremely difficult to see what he could do about it.

Could he double back into the Pacific?

With what object? All German possessions in the area were now in Allied hands, and he would need fuel just as much in the South Seas as in the Atlantic. If the German inhabitants of the scattered islands had coal—which was extremely unlikely—they certainly had no shipping in which it could meet him.

He *must* go on—but what with the weather, the sight of coal disappearing overboard from practically every ship in the squadron, his own not particularly intricate calculations, and now the fundamental uncertainty raised by this telegram, it seemed that he had better not ignore any other source of fuel which might contribute to his needs—whatever the risks entailed in collecting it. As his ships fought their way southward against grudging elements which exacted an extortionate price in energy and fuel for every mile forward it allowed the squadron to creep, von Spee turned back to a further consideration of an attack upon the Falkland Islands.

Von Knorr had brought with him from Coronel the same rumour as had Captain Ebeling from Punta Arenas, and with the news that the coal supply off Pernambuco was in jeopardy, von Spee had already taken the precaution of starting a check upon the reliability of that rumour. When *Amasis* had left Penas Gulf for Cape Virgins, her commander, Lieutenant zur Helle, had been instructed to probe the whole matter as deeply as he could, and if he thought that the Falklands *had* been abandoned, he was also to discover if the coal stocks at Port Stanley had been fired or not.

With the situation developing as it was, it looked as though the fate of von Spee's command might hang upon the news which zur Helle gave him upon arrival on the east coast. If zur Helle were satisfied that there was no defence worth considering on the Falkland Islands, then perhaps after all the idea of a descent upon the British possession might bear reconsideration—whatever the actual coal position at Port Santa Elena. Politically it would undoubtedly have wide repercussions, and tactically as well for if the only British base off the south coast of America could be rendered unserviceable by the destruction of its arsenal, wireless station and stores, then the position of whatever British Naval Forces there were in the neighbourhood would be weakened, and his own position proportionately strengthened. If the British stores and fuel moreover, were to find their way into his own holds and bunkers, then his resultant independence of the supply bases in South America could give him a freedom of movement which might, in the final issue, prove decisive.

But supposing zur Helle was not satisfied that the rumour was true—what then? What naval forces could there be at Port Stanley to dispute his occupation of the island? *Canopus* might be there and perhaps *Glasgow*. *Carnarvon*, *Cornwall* and *Bristol* were all—according to the intelligence he had received—somewhere in the South Atlantic, but the only ship he knew of which would constitute a threat of real weight and menace was *Defence*. Where was she?

The problem began to resolve itself—as do a large number which deal with matters of human behaviour—into one of bookmaker's odds. Was it likely that on the day von Spee descended upon the islands, all British naval shipping in the area would be concentrated in Port Stanley harbour?

Hardly—and the project began already to look a little more attractive.

Was it likely that all British naval shipping in the South Atlantic would even be within a day's steaming? Unlikely. Two days' steaming? Unlikely but possible. Three days' steaming? Possible —but if von Spee could secure possession of the island in their absence, then the enemy ships, having heard the news, would have to concentrate before launching a counter-attack. This would take time, during which he might contrive to slip away.

In any case, if it was unlikely that all British naval shipping in the area would be together in Port Stanley, it was also unlikely that it would *all* be at sea. Even granted that the British had learned at Coronel the necessity of concentration, there were always matters of maintenance and repairs. Suppose that he caught *Canopus* and say, one County class cruiser in harbour, he should have comparatively little difficulty in disposing of them and would then be only liable to attack by the residue.

Such a division of forces would undoubtedly be the best that he could hope for should the rumour of abandonment of the islands be completely untrue : the worst would be to meet the entire squadron during the approaches to the islands. Even then—as long as *Defence* was not present—the East Asiatic Squadron would be faced with an enemy only slightly stronger than he had been at Coronel, although if *Canopus* were present the action must be fought at a range outside that of her 12-inch guns. The issue even then would surely not be in doubt, and the East Asiatic Squadron would have struck yet another glorious blow for the Fatherland. Moreover, they may then have available the dockyard facilities at Port Stanley for any repairs which might be necessary and possible, plus the coal supplies with which the British Admiralty intended to fuel their South Atlantic Squadron for months to come.

If their luck held, the squadron could well ignore the coal and provisions awaiting them at Port Santa Elena—whatever they amounted to—and start out from Port Stanley for the Canaries with full bunkers, although possibly with empty magazines. A better alternative than the reverse, and anyway a small enough price to pay for the virtual destruction of British prestige in the southern areas. Really, the project looked positively inviting.

But where was *Defence*? If she were encountered, could *Scharnhorst* and *Gneisenau* fight her with any chance of success? If she were not in the area, how many days—or hours—would von Spee have undisturbed in harbour? If his own ships were at all damaged in an action with a part of the enemy forces during the approach to the islands, could his men occupy and hold them against attack by the remainder?

The permutations and combinations of alternative situations which might face him were endless, but the steps which he could take to anticipate them all were not. Having once rounded the Horn, von Spee could either proceed to Port Santa Elena, or he could go to Port Stanley—and if he chose the former course of action and then found that the telegram from Buenos Aires had been substantially correct, he would not have sufficient fuel to reach the Canaries and an ignominious end would face him, probably without an enemy unit in sight at which to strike a dying blow. Internment in a neutral country for the duration of the war was not a prospect to be accepted while any alternative remained. The nearer the squadron drew to the Falkland Islands, the more attractive they seem to have appeared.

All through the closing days of November, the squadron laboured south, but at last, on 1 December, the gale showed signs of moderating. They were now off the southern, island-studded coast of Tierra del Fuego—the land 'stark with eternal cold'— steaming east-south-east across a beam sea. It became possible to clear away some of the storm wreckage, to dry out clothing and blankets, eventually to prepare hot food in the galleys. It also became possible to re-assess the fuel position and draw up reports upon the effect the gale had had on the steaming abilities of the individual ships.

It was as a result of this investigation that *Dresden*, on the morning of 2 December, informed the Admiral that she had not enough coal aboard to make Cape dos Bahias and Santa Elena. The signal she received in reply was to the effect that she would be given a chance to coal *en route*—probably at the Falkland Islands.

It looks as though von Spee had made his decision.

The squadron passed an enormous iceberg during the morning

—which excited great interest among the crews—and they at last rounded the Horn at about noon in the middle of a hailstorm. Had they steamed straight on, they would have been at Port Stanley by 5 December—when Sturdee and his battle-cruisers were still two days' steaming away. They would have met opposition from the guns of *Canopus* and the anti-invasion forces marshalled under Captain Heathcote Grant, but it is questionable whether these would have been sufficient to drive them off. As the wireless station would doubtless have reported their presence before it had been shelled into silence, it is thus extremely likely that the ships of the East Asiatic Squadron would then have been caught by Sturdee in Stanley Harbour like rats in a trap.

But Fate had other ideas.

As the squadron approached Staten Island, a sailing-vessel was seen creeping westward between themselves and the coast. After investigation, the *Leipzig* reported her to be the Canadian-owned *Drummuir*, carrying 2,800 tons of Cardiff coal to San Francisco. It was a cargo too valuable to be ignored and no one could as yet divine the part which time was playing in their affairs. The squadron wheeled and made for the sheltered waters of the Beagle Channel. At 5 a.m. on 3 December, they anchored in about twenty-eight fathoms of water, off the east coast of Picton Island.

Coaling began immediately.

A study of the accounts of the East Asiatic Squadron's stay at Picton Island and of the events which followed almost immediately upon their departure, offers an illuminating example of what can happen to a commander-in-chief who receives instructions but not intelligence. There was so much that von Spee did not know— and in view of the vaunting reputation which German intelligence organizations were to be accorded during the remainder of the war and especially during the years which immediately followed it, it is interesting to see how dismally they failed at least one of their Admirals.

La Plata knew by 24 November that *Canopus* was guarding Port Stanley, and that some of her guns had been mounted in batteries ashore. La Plata also knew that a British squadron had been sighted three hundred miles from Montevideo on 22 November, and most important of all they had received a report that *Invincible* had been at Abrolhos on 26 November. Yet the best they could do to pass this information to the only person to whom it was vitally important, was to enclose it with other reports which would await him at Port Santa Elena—some six hundred miles past the only base in southern waters from which these forces could be operating.

Von Spee was not even to know for certain that *any* worthwhile intelligence would be awaiting him at Port Santa Elena and he had been quite definitely misled regarding coal supplies, for despite the telegram, seven thousand tons had been despatched to the rendezvous together with most of the stores and provisions which he had requested in his original instructions. In addition, there was a telegram from the Naval Staff awaiting him there. It was dated 1 December and read : 'Where shall the ammunition vessels be sent to? They will be ready for sea by the second half of December.'

There was thus no real need for him even to have considered a descent upon the Falkland Islands—as indeed he had concluded in the early days at Penas Gulf. Had it not been for that telegram from Buenos Aires—surely impelled by panic—he would possibly not have gone near the place.

His ships flew no flags at Picton Island, and officers who went ashore conversed deliberately with two of the inhabitants in English—a small bluff but to no avail, for despite their assurances to the contrary, they were bluntly informed that one of the light cruisers was *Bremen* (she had called there some years before and was similar to *Leipzig*) and the two inhabitants also let it clearly be seen that they had a shrewd idea as to the identities of the armoured cruisers.

Only forty miles away, at Ushuaia on the north side of the channel, was a trading station with a wireless-telegraphy installation—so von Spee must at least have suspected that his position would be reported to the world within a few days, and quite possibly within a few hours. He certainly had no further reason to hope that any descent upon Port Stanley by his ships would hold the immense advantage of surprise.

Yet little sense of urgency seems to have animated the squadron. *Drummuir*'s cargo was emptied into *Baden* and *Santa Isabel*, while *Seydlitz* went alongside *Dresden*. In due course, all cruisers topped up their bunkers and renewed their deck cargoes, and it was 6 December before they were ready to put to sea again—by which time they were four days behind on their schedule.

In the forenoon before they left, von Spee called a meeting of captains aboard the flagship and announced—according to the official German accounts : 'that in the absence of further reports he might possibly carry out an attack on the Falklands in order to destroy the wireless station and the arsenal, and also to take the Governor prisoner as a measure of retaliation for the imprisonment and inconsiderate treatment of the Governor of Samoa.' This last reason strikes an odd note, for von Spee does not seem to have been a person easily influenced by propaganda or much swayed by trivialities—and as such he would almost certainly have regarded the discomfiture of a political nominee.

Whatever the real reasons for the proposed attack, however, it quickly became obvious at the meeting of captains that opinion upon its advisability was by no means unanimous. The Chief of Staff, Captain Fielitz, and von Schönberg of *Nürnberg* supported the idea, but the other captains thought that a far more advisable course would be to circle wide around the islands, passing them some hundred miles to the east, and then to proceed to Port Santa Elena where some provisions, news and intelligence at least should await them, if not as much as was hoped for.

Von Spee however—whether he had completely made up his own mind or not—was not to be moved by anything like a majority decision, and he instructed Captain Maerker of *Gneisenau* to draw up plans for an attack on Port Stanley, based on the assumption that it would be carried out by his own ship and *Nürnberg* while the other ships of the squadron waited below the horizon as a reserve, upon which to fall back should any serious opposition be encountered. In view of the lack of information, this was probably as good a scheme as any—although he might have been well advised to instruct Captain Maerker to plan an approach to the islands from some other direction than the most obvious. Possibly he thought such an instruction was unnecessary, and was then loath to interfere when the plan was presented.

As the squadron left Picton Island, eight fires were seen suddenly to appear along the north coast—and as his command consisted of five warships and three colliers, von Spee could have had little doubt upon their significance. Any cautionary effect which they might have had, however, was dispelled during the night by the arrival at last of a signal from Lieutenant zur Helle on *Amasis*. It stated that as far as could be ascertained, the rumour of abandonment of the islands still seemed very likely to be true and that there was neither evidence nor even rumour to suggest that the coal stocks had been fired or any other destruction carried out.

The die was cast.

During the morning of 7 December, Captain Maerker drew up and issued his orders for the attack on Port Stanley by *Gneisenau* and *Nürnberg*. They are interesting in their brevity :

When *Gneisenau* and *Nürnberg* are detached on 8 December, they will proceed at fourteen knots to a point to the east of Cape Pembroke from which Port Stanley can be overlooked. If the harbour is clear of enemy ships, *Nürnberg* will reconnoitre as far north as Berkeley Sound, while *Gneisenau* off Port William lowers boats to sweep the entrance clear of mines.

Nürnberg will then proceed in as far as Port Stanley in rear of boats, and will embark stores and do destruction. *Gneisenau* will follow as far as the channel connecting Port William and Port Stanley. She will anchor there and send armed cutters to the townside under command of Lieutenant Kotthaus, who is to deliver an ultimatum to the Governor and try to bring him back to the ship. The cutters will be covered by *Nürnberg*. The two ships will rejoin the squadron not later than 7 p.m.

Possibly translation is responsible for its rather perfunctory tone and of course operation orders are not usually written for posterity, but it does seem that Captain Maerker lavished little in the way of subtlety or even imagination upon the order—perhaps because he considered these qualities unnecessary. It certainly does not read like the plan of a man who was enamoured of the project it covered and when, later in the day, he requested that a second light cruiser be assigned to him as outpost vessel, von Spee replied that the whole squadron would follow in, fifteen miles to the rear, and then take up position outside the harbour.

Whether this move had been in the Admiral's mind all the time cannot be stated, but the announcement was made just before a lengthy signal was sent from *Scharnhorst* to the large auxiliary *Elinore Woermann*, by now awaiting him at Port Santa Elena. The German official account suggests that this message was merely to inform the auxiliary of the delay in arrival of the Cruiser Squadron, but it would hardly take a lengthy signal to do that, and it has been suggested (though never, as far as can be ascertained, proved) that this signal ordered the captain of the *Elinore Woermann* to secure large stocks of barbed wire, entrenching tools and cement, and be ready to sail immediately upon receipt of orders to do so.

Another rumour which is quoted by practically all British accounts of the situation is that a German sheep-breeder of ancient lineage resident in Chile named Baron von Maltzahn, was instructed about this time to gather around him a force of about five hundred compatriots to undertake temporary garrison duties in an area which remained unspecified but which for reasons geographical, political and strategical could hardly have been in doubt. The apparent absurdity of such a scheme diminishes somewhat when it is remembered that von Spee was operating against very high odds, and that only by the fullest exploitation of every opportunity could he hope for any degree of success at all. The Falkland Islands under German occupation—however temporary—could prove of tactical value and would undoubtedly be a shattering blow to British prestige.

It did not become dark on the evening of Monday, 7 December, until nearly 11.30 p.m. British time (German time was half an hour earlier), and in those latitudes at the end of the year, night only lasts some three hours. As early as 2.30 a.m.—according to the accounts of *Gneisenau*'s executive officer—land masses were seen to northwards, and the squadron steamed steadily towards them with *Dresden* about two miles in the lead. At 5.30 a.m., *Scharnhorst* hoisted the signal to detach, and *Gneisenau* and *Nürnberg* increased speed to come past her and forge ahead. They were intended to be off Cape Pembroke by 8.30 a.m.

For those latitudes it was a perfect summer morning. The sea was calm, the sky high and clear, but the air temperature only in the forties : there would be no heat haze to obscure or distort the distant view. The barometer was steady and the light north-westerly breeze fresh enough to sharpen the delight in life and in strength.

It was a day for great deeds.

By six o'clock it had become possible to take bearings on features along the southern shore of East Falkland and from the results it was found that *Gneisenau* and *Nürnberg* would not be off Cape Pembroke before 9.30 a.m. (British time). The flagship was informed and the two ships increased speed still further. At 8.30 a.m. the tops of the wireless masts became visible and soon afterwards the lighthouse at Cape Pembroke was sighted.

Then at 8.40 a.m. a column of smoke was seen passing behind the lighthouse to the westwards—into harbour—and as the neck of land guarding Port Stanley from the south came into view, the masts of several vessels were seen rising above it. It seems that for a brief second the startled first lieutenant of the *Gneisenau* saw a battle-cruiser's tripod masts through his binoculars, but smoke was rising in dense columns from behind the low hills and they presently merged into one thick cloud. The first lieutenant was told rather brusquely that there were no battle-cruisers nearer than the Mediterranean, and the general opinion on the bridge was that the density of the smoke was due to the firing of coal and oil stocks.

Gneisenau and *Nürnberg* steamed on. The wireless-station must be shelled into silence as quickly as possible, but by 9 a.m. it was obvious that there were a number of warships in the harbour, and

Captain Maerker calculated that there were probably two ships of *Kent*'s class, two of *Glasgow*'s class and possibly two bigger ships like *Canopus*. He kept his Admiral informed of these conclusions and steamed onwards.

The upper works of the ship proceeding into harbour (it was the guard ship *Macedonia*) could now clearly be seen, and so could the three funnels and two masts of a *Kent* class cruiser moving in the opposite direction—out to sea. Excitement ran through the German ships together with no little jubilation, for the first lieutenant now kept his fears to himself (as did one or two others whose glasses had been pointing momentarily in the right direction) and there was little doubt aboard that the success of Coronel was about to be repeated.

Then at 9.20 a.m. two huge mushrooms rose out of the sea some thousand yards to port, then came the sounds the shells had made through the air and eventually the heavy thumps of the discharging guns. There could be no doubt that they were now under heavy calibre fire, though the guns themselves remained completely invisible, and Captain Maerker turned his ships slightly away to the eastward, ordered them cleared for action and hoisted his battle-ensigns. Two more mushrooms rose, again the booming of heavy artillery reached them but the shells were still well short. The British cruiser coming out to sea was at this point definitely recognized as *Kent*.

Gneisenau moved in to cut her off—for it was considered that she was probably trying to escape. Hardly had Captain Maerker steadied on the closing course however, when a signal was received from von Spee. It read :

Do not accept action. Concentrate on course east by south. Proceed at full speed.

Shortly afterwards the Admiral ordered all ships to raise full steam in all boilers.

It was now 9.50 a.m.

Gneisenau and *Nürnberg* turned right away from the island (another shot from *Canopus* was aimed at *Gneisenau*'s rapidly departing stern) and *Scharnhorst*, *Dresden* and *Leipzig* gathered speed along a course practically due east, some twelve miles south of, and parallel to, the length of Stanley Harbour. It was now seen that there was considerable movement in the harbour. Smoke was still pouring upwards from at least half a dozen points and now those points of origin were moving—and with movement the dense smoke clouds tended to disperse.

Still on the German ships there seems to have been little premonition of extreme danger. There was even some murmured disappointment that the Admiral seemed to have decided that discretion was the better part of valour, especially in view of the fact that he had already told Captain von Schultze that he really thought very little of the squadron's chances of arriving safely in home waters. If the Admiral really held this opinion, then why not accept battle here and now—and deliver yet another shattering blow to Britain's Navy and prestige?

But possibly it was in the Admiral's mind to lure the British ships to sea, destroy them there, and then return and occupy the island?

The murmurings were silenced, confidence rose.

Then at 10 a.m., quite clearly and distinctly, two officers aboard the *Leipzig* saw a pair of tripod masts moving towards the outer harbour entrance, and when, whitefaced, they sought each other's opinion, they made the additionally horrifying discovery that they had not both been looking at the same pair.

Two battle-cruisers—a completely overwhelming force!

They tried—so one of them was later to relate—frantically to disbelieve the evidence of their own eyes.

CHAPTER EIGHT

THERE was once a young man of Cape Horn, who wished he had never been born, and had he been present in Port Stanley at about half-past eight on that Tuesday morning, 8 December 1914, he would—according to Lieutenant-Commander Verner—have merely been one among many. At this time it appeared to officers and men of Admiral Sturdee's command that they were in a most awkward situation.

Both *Invincible* and *Inflexible* still had colliers alongside from which they had each managed to whip aboard but four hundred tons of coal (about one seventh of their capacity) and although *Carnarvon*, *Glasgow* and *Bristol* had managed to take aboard their quota, the last two were right inside the inner harbour (where, moreover, *Bristol* had her fires drawn for boiler repairs) and *Carnarvon* in the outer harbour still had her decks stacked with coal, which in an immediate action could cause more casualties among her own crew than enemy ammunition. *Cornwall*, *Kent* and *Macedonia* had not even begun coaling, and the first-named had an engine opened up at six hours' notice.

The squadron was thus hardly in a position to repel a determined attack from an enemy of proved fighting ability and courage —and should that enemy press home the attack to the very mouth of the harbour, then the position of the British ships inside would be precarious indeed.

Even when it was realized that the main body of the enemy was twenty miles away and his nearest force still eight miles distant, there was good reason for alarm, for only *Glasgow*, *Kent* and *Macedonia* were not right in the middle of some vital operation and of these only *Glasgow* could be counted fit and ready for an extended sea action. Even she would need two hours to develop full steam pressure.

The look-out on Sapper Hill had first seen the smoke and then the masts of the approaching *Gneisenau* at 7.35 a.m. By 7.45 a.m., *Canopus* had received the message 'A four-funnel and a two-funnel* man-of-war in sight steering northwards' by telephone from the post, and as *Canopus* was screened from the flagship by low hills, *Glasgow* was used as repeating ship. The battle-cruisers being both fully engaged in coaling, Captain Luce of *Glasgow* ordered a gun fired at 7.56 a.m. to draw attention to the signal 'Enemy in sight' flying from his halliards, and a few moments before eight o'clock, the flag lieutenant aboard *Invincible* burst in upon Admiral Sturdee as he was shaving, to tell him the momentous news.

According to one unconfirmed report, Admiral Sturdee replied with the traditional, 'Then send the men to breakfast'. Whether he did or not, there is reason to believe that little food was consumed aboard the ships of his command during the ensuing hour. Disbelief that the enemy would come so obligingly to meet them, thus saving them all a long and probably wearisome search, was followed first by astonishment at the apparent good luck which was attending the squadron, and then almost immediately by a startled consideration of whether the good luck was, in fact, on their side.

Swift review and reflection aroused ominous doubts. If von Spee was really determined to fight a battle with the British forces now in Port Stanley, he could hardly attack them under more favourable conditions for himself than those which now existed. Accurate salvoes from the heavier armament of *Scharnhorst* and *Gneisenau* (and *Glasgow* at least knew just how accurate those salvoes could be) might severely damage even the heavily armoured

Nürnberg, which actually had three funnels.

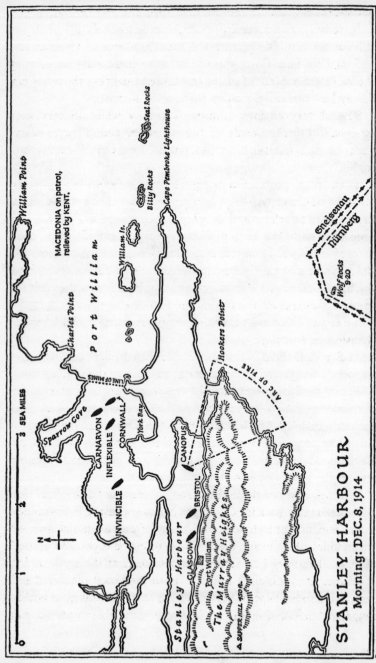

STANLEY HARBOUR
Morning: DEC.8, 1914

© CASSELL & CO. LTD. 1960.

0   1   2   3 SEA MILES

N

William Point

MACEDONIA on patrol,
relieved by KENT.

Port William

Charles Point

William Is.

Billy Rocks

Cape Pembroke Lighthouse

Seal Rocks

Gneisenau
Nürnberg

Wolf Rocks
9.20

LINE OF MINES

Sparrow Cove

CARNARVON
INFLEXIBLE
INVINCIBLE
CORNWALL

York Bay

Hookers Point

ARC OF FIRE

Stanley Harbour

GLASGOW
BRISTOL
CANOPUS

Port William
The Murray Heights

SAPPER HILL 450 ft.

battle-cruisers, and in the confined spaces of the harbour it was only too likely that some British ships would mask the fire of others. Add to the resulting picture the possible effects of German torpedoes, fired from ships whose crews were consciously immolating themselves in a blaze of glory, and those visualizing the scene can hardly be blamed for wishing themselves elsewhere.

Several very anxious minutes ticked by while all ears were strained for exact details of the situation, and all eyes above decks were on the flagship to learn what steps were to be taken to ease it.

Then at 8.10 a.m., bunting fluttered from *Invincible*'s halliards. *Kent* was ordered to weigh and proceed out through the mine-barrier both to relieve and possibly to protect the *Macedonia*, and also to observe the enemy. Four minutes later, all ships were ordered to prepare to weigh and captains were to report how soon their ships could have steam up. Engine and boiler-rooms became the scenes of frantic activity, fires were lit and forced and black smoke belched from the funnels to wrap the upper works in the dense cloud which might well be considered to have saved many British lives that day.

At 8.30 a.m. 'Action' was sounded, the colliers cast off, and Sapper Hill reported more smoke visible above the horizon away to the south-west. *Gneisenau* and *Nürnberg* were now making for the wireless-station, and as the configuration of the land masked the opposing forces from each other, the position of the German ships was constantly reported from the observation post. As yet Captains Maerker and von Schönberg had not seen the rising smoke, the tell-tale masts.

Kent passed down the harbour and out towards Cape Pembroke, *Macedonia* came back in, *Cornwall*'s engineers hastily re-assembled their dismantled machinery, and aboard *Canopus*, the stokers off watch climbed up inside the foremost funnel and perched around the top, determined to secure the best seats at the forthcoming spectacle. At nine o'clock Captain Heathcote Grant requested and received permission to open fire as soon as the enemy came within range, and in case it should be necessary or possible to get his ship to sea, he ordered her boilers to be lit. Disgusted, the off-watch stokers came down again.

Gneisenau and *Nürnberg* steamed on (about this time the former's first lieutenant was discovering that despite his Captain's rebuke, some of his fellow officers also believed they had seen tripod masts) and a quarter of an hour later they were at the Wolf Rocks, swinging round to present their broadsides to the wireless-station. As they did so, officers in the observation post ashore saw the landing-parties assembled on *Gneisenau*'s decks through the lenses of their instruments, and as the ranges came through to the gunnery officer aboard *Canopus*, Captain Heathcote Grant gave the order to open fire.

When the two 12-inch guns of the fore-turret responded with the first shots of the battle, it was exactly 9.20 a.m. Twelve grim hours were to pass before the battle ended.

Aboard *Inflexible*, Lieutenant-Commander Verner was seeking vainly for some way in which to bring his gun-crews into action. From his position in the fore-top he had an excellent view of the advance force of the enemy, now some eighteen thousand yards away, but he had no director-finding equipment, and from the gun-decks below all that was visible was the sandy, rock-strewn peninsula leading out to Cape Pembroke. Steam-pressure would not be high enough for the ship to move for another hour, and *Scharnhorst*, *Dresden* and *Leipzig* were already visible coming up fast over the horizon; if *Gneisenau* and *Nürnberg* failed to block the harbour, then the remainder of the German squadron could still close the far side of the peninsula, where they would be in an ideal position from which to enfilade the British ships as they came out.

Then *Canopus* fired again, and *Gneisenau* and *Nürnberg* turned east out of range of her guns, turning back in again at 9.31 a.m. to intercept *Kent*, by now abreast of Pembroke Lighthouse. As Admiral Sturdee recalled *Kent*, von Spee's instructions to Captain Maerker not to accept action must have been received aboard the *Gneisenau*, for the German ships turned away. If the manœuvre was inexplicable to the British who watched it nevertheless afforded them considerable relief.

Inside Port Stanley and Port William Harbours, the efforts of the engine-room staffs were now beginning to show results as indictators moved point by point up the pressure gauges. *Glasgow* shortened in her cable, weighed and came through the outer harbour to join *Kent*, Admiral Stoddart was ordered to clear *Carnarvon* for action and proceed to sea, and at ten o'clock the battle-cruisers at last left their anchorages and passed out through the gap in the minefield, followed shortly by *Cornwall*. As they swept down towards Cape Pembroke, *Glasgow* reported the enemy steaming away to the south-east as hard as they could go.

Visibility was at its maximum. The sea was calm, the sky clear and pale, and a cold north-westerly breeze wrapped the ships in their own smoke. As *Invincible* cleared Cape Pembroke, Sturdee ordered the signal 'General Chase' to be hoisted, and few aboard his ships who saw it could have failed to have been reminded of historical precedent. 'No more glorious moment ... do I remember in the war than this!' Lieutenant Hirst was to write years later, and indeed the violent tensions of the last few hours—for men of *Glasgow* the culmination of the weeks of unhappiness since Coronel—were released in the wave of confidence which now surged through the squadron.

The long line of British ships stretched eastward from the harbour with *Glasgow* far ahead in the lead. Then came *Invincible* and *Cornwall*—and fifteen miles to the south-east the two groups of enemy ships were drawing together. Dense smoke still poured from the funnels of all ships as they forced their engines up to maximum power, and the battle-cruisers crept inexorably on towards the head of the line. They formed a sight which has lived in the memories of all who watched: 12-inch guns trained on the enemy on a forward bearing, bow waves curling away whitely from the stems and the seas astern mounded up almost to the height of the after decks. Speed and striking-power were implicit in the clean lines of hull and upperworks, and aloft against the thick oil-dark mass of their smoke, battle-ensigns fluttered as vivid as lance-pennants.

Excitement and anticipation filled the fleet with vital force, stamping the scene indelibly into the consciousness of everyone present.

At 10.48 a.m. *Glasgow* reported that the enemy ships were now only twelve miles ahead, and as it seemed that they were not steaming at more than eighteen knots while the battle-cruisers and the *Glasgow* were making over twenty-four, it was reasonable to assume that no escape would be possible for the German ships. It was also reasonable for Admiral Sturdee to decide that with the rest of the long Antarctic day before him, he had no need to force an immediate action. He therefore ordered a reduction of speed of his leading ships, both to allow his County class cruisers to come up and also to try to lessen the pall of smoke which wreathed his ships and would undoubtedly hamper the gun-layers when action was joined. By 11.15 a.m., the speed of the British squadron was down to nineteen knots with *Glasgow* keeping station three miles ahead of *Invincible*, while *Inflexible* had come round on the flag-ship's starboard quarter. *Kent* was some two miles astern and *Carnarvon* and *Cornwall* as much again.

Glasgow still reported both the enemy positions and their movements.

By now they were well in sight from the flagship, their funnels and bridges above the horizon and according to calculation their speed was down to fifteen knots. Their course so far had been almost due east, but suddenly von Spee was seen to turn his ships away to starboard. At 11.25 a.m., the British altered together and the two squadrons were again on parallel but now south-easterly courses.

At 11.30 a.m. Sturdee ordered that hands should be sent to dinner. He also turned two more points to starboard to put his ships on to a converging course, and then had his attention tem-porarily recalled to his base. At about 10.30 a.m., von Spee's three colliers, the *Seydlitz*, *Baden* and *Santa Isabel* had approached Port Pleasant—a small creek about thirty miles south of Port Stanley—

and were there observed by the occupants of the only dwelling in the vicinity. These occupants were a Mrs Felton, a small boy and a maid. Stationing herself on a top of the nearest high ground and her maid at the cottage telephone, Mrs Felton warned Captain Heathcote Grant of the presence of the enemy ships and kept him supplied with details of their movements, the small boy bounding between the two ladies bearing information and reply, all in the best tradition of Captain Marryat and Max Pemberton.

All this time, the unfortunate *Bristol* had been trying to get to sea. Due to magnificent efforts on the part of her engineers, steam had been raised in record time and she had at last come out into Port William, clearing the harbour by 10.50 a.m. As she did so, Captain Grant passed to her the information regarding the colliers, which in turn Captain Fanshawe endeavoured to pass to the flagship. Until 11.20 a.m. however, he was prevented from doing so by enemy wireless jamming, but upon eventually establishing contact he immediately received orders from his Admiral to join forces with the armed liner *Macedonia* and 'attack and destroy the transports', for in view of the rumours of the gathering together in Chilean ports of German nationals to form garrison parties, Admiral Sturdee concluded that such these auxiliaries must be.

Few men on the ships of his command ate their dinner in the confines of their messdecks. In an atmosphere of intense excitement and confidence, they lined the upper decks with hastily and unusually constituted sandwiches, eagerly discussing the approaching action. Few of them had ever heard a shot fired in anger before, and all had been raised on the belief that the Royal Navy was invincible. Only those aboard *Glasgow* had much idea of the realities of a naval battle. Lieutenant-Commander Verner, in the foretop of the *Inflexible*, having made certain that all his communications were working effectively, was far more concerned about the possibility of the flagship's smoke blinding his gun-layers than he was about possible damage to *Inflexible*, her gun-crews or himself. Like most of the professional seamen aboard he saw the opportunity before him as one in which to test his long-cherished theories of naval warfare and seems to have been far more interested in observing the effects of shell-fire, even on the hull and upper-works of his own ship, then he was in the actual sinking of the enemy—although he would have been the first to state that this was, in fact, the object of the exercise.

By noon it had become evident that the old *Carnarvon*—Admiral Stoddart's flagship—could not maintain the necessary speed to catch up with the rest of the British squadron, and *Cornwall* was ordered to leave her and come forward. Then at 12.20 p.m. von Spee's squadron was seen to be changing formation and again altering to starboard. British crews were ordered to their stations, *Inflexible* opened up to five cables on the flagship's quarter and speed was again picked up to twenty-five knots.

At 12.50 p.m., by which time the enemy were hull up, the general order to engage was given. Seven minutes later *Inflexible* fired her opening round at *Leipzig*, whose tired and overstrained engines could not keep her up with the rest of the squadron. The shell fell well short, and so did the second one fired at extreme elevation, for 16,000 yards was too much even for the guns of the battle-cruisers. *Invincible* opened fire a few minutes later, but of the twelve shells fired at *Leipzig* in this opening brush, only three landed within a hundred yards of her—although one fell ahead and she was lost to sight as she steamed on through the splash.

There was now a short pause in the firing while *Glasgow* and the battle-cruisers inexorably closed the gap between themselves and the quarry—and during it von Spee took the decision which entitles him to our greatest respect. At 1.20 p.m. he hoisted the signal 'Light cruisers part company and endeavour to escape'. This was followed almost immediately by instructions to *Gneisenau* to turn, and with the *Scharnhorst*, to accept action. As he took his two armoured cruisers around to the north-east, von Spee might have wondered if his old friend Cradock was watching him.

Invincible and *Inflexible* turned seven points to port, and without a signal being passed, *Glasgow* doubled back down their dis-engaged side and bore off to the southward after the fleeing light cruisers, with *Kent* and *Cornwall* in company. *Carnarvon*, now ten miles astern, altered course to cut the corner and try to come up with the flagship.

As at Coronel by six o'clock in the evening, the main forces were now ranging broadside against broadside—but this time there were still at least eight hours of daylight left and there were no mounting seas or storm clouds to add their uncertainties to the hazards of war. At 1.30 p.m., across a calm sea and under an untroubled sky, the first broadside salvoes were fired—*Invincible* against *Gneisenau*, *Inflexible* against *Scharnhorst*.

The British line had fired first at a range of 14,500 yards, and as the spotting-officers and range-finders watched for the fall of shot, twinkles of light and brown smears of smoke appeared on the quarterdeck and forecastles of the enemy. In *Inflexible*'s fore-top there was a second's interested silence, broken when someone said in tones of shocked incredulity, 'They're firing at us!' Then white mushrooms rose out of the sea short of the enemy line, and as another neater group of mushrooms did so some thousand yards away, the men of the *Inflexible* heard for the first time the scream of enemy shell.

The lines converged, the British guns fired again and from his platform Lieutenant-Commander Verner noted a long low wall of water rise to the level of *Scharnhorst*'s upper deck. So that was what an under-water hit looked like. It happened again after *Inflexible*'s third salvo, but then *Scharnhorst* passed in front of *Gneisenau* to lead the German line and the British battle-cruisers changed targets.

At 1.45 p.m. *Invincible* was hit—not apparently as a result of a straddling salvo but by a single shell at the limit of the German ranges—and like von Spee at Coronel, Sturdee edged his ships away into the penumbra between the ranges of the opposing guns. Unlike von Spee at Coronel however, he did not have the advantage of wind or sun, and on the new bearing the battle-cruisers' smoke drifted down towards the enemy so that *Inflexible*'s guns were completely blinded, as were those of the flagship aft of the fore-turret. As a result of this movement away from the enemy and the smoke interference, the ranges imperceptibly opened out until by two o'clock the lines were sixteen thousand yards apart again and firing ceased.

At this time, *Kent*—having been left behind by *Glasgow* and *Cornwall* in the dash southwards after the light cruisers—was about four miles astern of the German ships and crossing their wake. Those aboard had thus enjoyed a superb view of the battle of the giants so far, and her commander, Captain Allen, has recorded this description of the developing scene :

> With the sun still shining on them, the German ships looked as if they had been painted for the occasion. They fired as if they had but eight minutes in which to make a record battle-practice score and never have I seen heavy guns fired with such rapidity and yet with such control. Flash after flash travelled down their sides from head to stern, all their six- and eight-inch guns firing every salvo.
>
> Of the British battle-cruisers less could be seen as their smoke drifted from them across the range and not only obscured their own view but also the spectator's view of them. Nevertheless, they seemed to be firing incessantly, their shells hitting the German ships at intervals whereas all that could be seen of the German fire was that it straddled the British ships. Four or five times in the first twenty minutes, the white puff of bursting shell could be seen among the clouds of brown cordite smoke on *Gneisenau*, and she was seen to be on fire near her mainmast, but this soon disappeared.
>
> By some trick of the wind the sounds were inaudible and the view was of silent combat, the two lines of ships steaming away to the east. Then just as *Kent* was completely astern of the Germans, they altered course away from the battle-cruisers a few points, suddenly to whip around parallel with *Kent* as though to attack her before the battle-cruisers could come to her rescue.

One can sympathize with Captain Allen in his interpretation of this sudden alteration of course, but it seems that von Spee's move was in fact a grasping of the only chance of escape which was offered him. Realizing that at this particular moment he must be completely invisible from the decks of the British heavy ships, he turned and fled southwards—where if his luck would change, he might find a cloud, a rain-squall, a bank of fog. But his movement was perceived, either by Sturdee through the smoke or (according to one source) by Admiral Stoddart still far behind the battle in the *Carnarvon*, who is thought then to have informed the flagship by wireless.

The battle-cruisers swung around and picked up speed again for another stern chase.

And at this moment, like a breath of peace and sanity from another age, another world, a full-rigged sailing ship passed silently on the port hand of the battle-cruisers, her white hull and sails bleached in the sunlight, and the clear air giving her a sparkling beauty which brought to the mind of one of her awestruck watchers the Tennysonian line, '. . . clothed in white samite, mystic, wonderful'. Almost he expected to hear Drake's Drum beating the long, compulsive roll, or to see the ship change shape to something squatter, wider, bluffer, and ports to swing up to the thunder of muzzle-loaders running out as Nelson's signal streamed from the mastheads. Then the moment was gone, the ship past. She was, according to Lieutenant Hirst, a Frenchman bound from Europe to Valparaiso, and as she had left port in July and carried no wireless, was unaware even that a war had broken out. Hoisting her colours, she went rapidly about and bore off to the northwards, her crew manning the yards to watch in some horror and astonishment as the battle-cruisers again raced after the enemy.

It was quite a long chase and during it some sober reflection was taking place aboard the British ships. Lieutenant-Commander Verner, for instance, discovered that his guns had already fired some hundred and fifty shells, for the expenditure of which he could only feel reasonably certain of three hits—and this in the ship which held the battle-practice championship. How many shells the enemy had fired was not known, but on every hand it was admitted that the German gunnery was first-class. The

Inflexible had not been hit, but the flagship had a hole in her side just forward of Q turret and she had also been hit exactly between the two guns of the fore-turret, denting but not piercing the armour. Owing to the extreme range at which the German guns were firing, their shells descended at something of the angle of the aerial bombs which were to spell disaster to the British battleships off the coast of Malaya in a later war, and although Sturdee could not have foreseen that catastrophe, he must have wondered what would happen if one of the superbly-grouped salvoes from the 8.2-inch guns ranged against him was to land together on his own unarmoured decks. Although the magazines were deep in the bowels of his ships, ammunition-hoists led directly up to the turrets, and shell exploding in the feed system could cause an explosion which might blow the heavily armoured sides of his battle-cruisers apart. At this range they were evidently more vulnerable from inside than out.

In addition to the gunnery of the ships who held the Kaiser's Gold Cup, there was the menace of their torpedoes—and in December 1914 the only experience which the Royal Navy had had of the effect of these weapons had been the sinking of *Aboukir*, *Hogue* and *Cressy* all within an hour on the morning of 22 September and that of *Hawke* on 15 October.

It behoved an Admiral who had thought for the value of his ships and the lives of the men aboard them, to act with all the caution which would still be commensurate with the final elimination of the enemy force. No avoidable risk must be run.

By 2.45 p.m. the range had closed again to 15,000 yards and fire was opened on the German ships once more. Lyddite shell was seen to burst on the after-deck of *Gneisenau*, and black hard-edged clouds suddenly belched from the *Scharnhorst*'s fore port casemates. Abruptly, the German ships turned nine points to port in succession and once again their broadsides flashed in unison. Aboard the British battle-cruisers, fascinated gunnery officers and spotters found themselves automatically working out the corrections of range and aim that their opponents should make in order to secure hits—an odd psychological reaction, but one which seems to take place in all naval actions—on both sides—so long as shots are falling short. Sturdee led around six points to port on to a course almost parallel but slightly convergent with the enemy line, and once again salvoes of 12-inch and 8·2-inch shells thundered from the opposing lines across the smooth, indifferent waves.

Gradually the range closed. By 3 p.m. it was down to 12,500 yards and still both Admirals held firmly on, broadside pounding against broadside—and now von Spee could bring his secondary armament into use. Aboard the British ships the noise was overwhelming. Enemy shells screamed shrilly overhead or burst violently in the water just short, sending up gouts of hissing water to wash angrily across the decks accompanied by the irritating hornet's whine of shell splinters; but above all, continuous, Homeric, all-engulfing, was the enormous crash and thunder of their own 12-inch salvoes. Again and again the huge guns roared out, their turrets occasionally swinging in response to correction like prehistoric animals blindly facing into danger, the long barrels slowly rising and falling like fingers or antennae reaching for prey. Then turrets and barrels would freeze into immobility, there might be an instant's precious silence, then eight orange jets of flame would burst forth, as long again as the barrels and wrapped in fury and a terrifying incandescence. As the guns recoiled the flames would lick onwards into dependent balls of fire transmuting themselves as they died into volumes of thick, chocolate-coloured smoke.

The smoke would rise slightly, mix with the black pall from the funnels, then descend and hang around the ships as though to wrap them fondly in a dense, protective cloud. Occasionally, as though to extend their protection, parts of the cloud would detach themselves and advance down the range towards the enemy, and although they effectively masked the target from the German gunners, they almost completely blinded the British as well. Lieutenant-Commander Verner in the fore-top of the *Inflexible* was almost the only man aboard his ship who could judge the whereabouts of the enemy, and as even he was handicapped by the

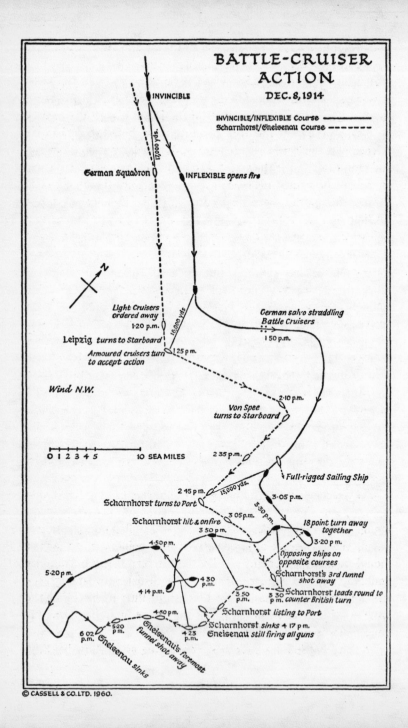

BATTLE-CRUISER ACTION

DEC. 8, 1914

INVINCIBLE/INFLEXIBLE Course ——————
Scharnhorst/Gneisenau Course ------------

INVINCIBLE

German Squadron

INFLEXIBLE *opens fire*

17,000 yds.

Light Cruisers
ordered away
1·20 p.m.

German salvo straddling
Battle Cruisers
1·50 p.m.

16,000 yds.

Leipzig turns to Starboard

Armoured cruisers turn
to accept action

1·25 p.m.

N

Wind N.W.

2·10 p.m.

Von Spee
turns to Starboard

2·35 p.m.

0 1 2 3 4 5   10 SEA MILES

Full-rigged Sailing Ship

2·45 p.m.   15,000 yds.

3·05 p.m.

Scharnhorst *turns to Port*

Scharnhorst *hit & on fire*

3·05 p.m.

3·50 p.m.

18 point turn away
together

3·20 p.m.

3·50 p.m.

Opposing ships on
opposite courses

4·50 p.m.

Scharnhorst's 3rd funnel
shot away

5·20 p.m.

4·30
p.m.

4·14 p.m.

3·50
p.m.

3·30
p.m.

Scharnhorst *leads round to
counter British turn*

Scharnhorst *listing to Port*

Scharnhorst *sinks* 4·17 p.m.

4·50 p.m.

5·20
p.m.

4·23
p.m.

Gneisenau *still firing all guns*

6·02
p.m.   Gneisenau *sinks*

Gneisenau's foremost
funnel shot away

smoke from the flagship ahead, he had great difficulty in assessing what damage his gunnery was causing—if any.

In addition to the smoke-nuisance, he was also handicapped—as was everyone else aboard—by the lack of war experience which ran through practically the whole of the Royal Navy. At one time he was puzzled by the lack of correlation between *Inflexible*'s salvoes and the shells which were undoubtedly bursting both on and closely alongside the target, and only the obvious effectiveness of the fire prevented his being seriously worried. It was not until the stem of another enemy ship crept into the right-hand edge of his field of vision, that he realized that he had been trying to spot *Inflexible*'s fire on *Invincible*'s target—a mistake of the type which is made once in the life of every marksman, whatever calibre weapon he uses.

At 3.20 p.m. Admiral Sturdee apparently decided that the smoke was making conditions completely intolerable for his gun-layers, and he gave orders for the battle-cruisers to turn away together eighteen points to port, so that they would double back across their own wakes on an opposite course to that of the enemy. With *Inflexible* leading, Verner was at last in a position from which he could watch the enemy and the effects of his own gunnery.

What surprised him most was the volume of fire which still came from a ship as badly battered as *Scharnhorst* could now be seen to be, for she had undoubtedly suffered tremendous damage. Her upper works were a torn and twisted shambles, her third funnel was gone, through huge gaps in her side blazing fires could be seen, and she was much lower in the water. Yet her salvoes, though more ragged than at first, were still well-grouped and fre-quent. When Sturdee ordered another four points turn to port as though to cross the enemy's wake, the German flagship promptly doubled back in a similar manner to the British turn (though she was followed in succession by *Gneisenau*, thus maintaining the same relative position in line), and this move brought her as yet unused starboard batteries into action.

The two battle-lines were now converging again, but this time

on a roughly westerly course and with the range closing to between 12,000 and 10,000 yards. While *Gneisenau* was following her
leader around, she had been lost to sight in the smoke and for a
short time *Scharnhorst* received the full attention of both battle-
cruisers. On *Inflexible*, Verner, astounded by the still almost perfect salvoes from the German flagship, ordered his crews to fire
'rapid independent' with the result that at one moment P turret
had three shells in the air, all of which were seen to land either on
target or near enough to cause damage.

Yet the German fire appeared unchecked. Clouds of steam
gushed upwards from the *Scharnhorst*'s decks, the first and second
funnels were leaning against each other, an enormous livid rent
had been torn in the side-plating below her quarterdeck and she
was blazing fore and aft—but still her starboard batteries fired
again and again.

Her masts were gone, her bridge was wrecked, her magazines
must have been almost empty and her boats reduced to match-
wood—but still her ensign fluttered from a jury mast above the
after-control station. Then suddenly, just before four o'clock, her
batteries ceased fire 'as when a light is blown out' and she was
seen to turn eight points to starboard and come staggering across
the seas directly at her powerful antagonists. Unknown at the time
to those who watched from the British decks, Admiral von Spee
was signalling *Gneisenau* to endeavour to escape if her engines
were still undamaged while *Scharnhorst* closed for a last desperate
attack with torpedoes—but by now far too many tons of water
were flooding the torn and riven hull of the flagship. Her bows
were dipping, her speed dropping and she listed heavily to
starboard.

Behind her, *Gneisenau* came into view firing rapidly and ac-
curately at *Inflexible*, and as Verner quickly shifted his fire to reply,
Invincible broke away from the line and headed across towards the
German flagship. Less than ten thousand yards separated the two
Admirals but it was soon evident that they would never meet, for
Scharnhorst's decks were a sea of fire and as her speed slackened
away, the list grew worse. Slower and slower she moved, further and

further she listed over as water flooded inboard and quenched the devouring flames. By 4.10 p.m., she was lying on her beam ends, her propellers turning idly above the lapping waves, steam and smoke billowing upwards from the stricken, mammoth shape. Through rents in her plating a few figures climbed laboriously and stood on her side-plates watching the battle-cruisers and the cold impartial sea.

It is not an Admiral's duty to save enemy lives while enemy units still fight. Whatever motives had sent Sturdee across the sea toward's von Spee's funeral-pyre, he could not risk the lives of *Inflexible*'s crew—still under fire from *Gneisenau*—while he saved possible survivors from *Scharnhorst*. As the German flagship lay on her side, and those of her complement who still lived faced the numbing paralysis of sudden immersion in icy waters after hours amid the flames, *Invincible* turned back to join the line astern of *Inflexible* and take up the battle again.

Scharnhorst lay above water for another seven minutes. Then, her propellers still turning as her bows went down and her stern came up, steam and smoke still wreathed about her and her flag still flying—she slid quickly forward under the water and was gone, leaving only a huge yellow patch on the surface of the sea, and a shimmering cloud above it.

Fifteen minutes later, *Carnarvon* reached the spot and steamed directly through the stained waters. Neither survivors nor wreckage was seen on either hand.

CHAPTER NINE

IT is possible to reconstruct the story of the part played by *Gneisenau* and her crew at the Battle of the Falkland Islands in more exact detail than that of the German flagship and her gallant Admiral and complement. It is certainly a story of which any ship or Navy might well be proud.

When Captain Maerker received the orders not to accept action with the *Kent* or any of the other ships in Port William, it must have been with a certain amount of vexation. He had been, it will be remembered, against the idea of an approach to the Falkland Islands in the first place, but it was one thing to avoid an enemy-held naval base altogether, and quite another to steam up to it—thus revealing to the enemy both one's position and strength—and then to steam away without attempting to reap the rewards which alone would justify such temerity.

However, in obedience to his orders he turned his back upon what he still believed to be an easy victory against inferior ships, and made off to the south-east on a course converging with that of his Admiral. By 11 a.m. (11.30 a.m. British time), *Gneisenau* and *Nürnberg* were some two thousand yards ahead of the German flagship, had turned to port on to the course of the main squadron and were slowing to allow them to catch up. The six British ships which had left Port Stanley in pursuit were some fifteen miles astern, and although they were constantly watched by all above decks, it was still with more interest than trepidation, for the battle-cruisers had not yet detached themselves from the line.

But if the majority of the officers and men of *Gneisenau* were still unaware of the trap into which they had strayed, those of *Leipzig* were under no illusions and their information had already been communicated to von Spee. He, by this time, was aware of the plight of his command, and his orders as the two sections of his squadron joined were that each ship was to proceed to the southeast at her maximum speed, irrespective of formation.

Gneisenau led, with *Nürnberg* keeping up bravely on her starboard quarter, and—very soon—*Dresden* up on her port beam. *Scharnhorst* still lay some five cables astern, just ahead and to port of the lagging *Leipzig*.

Gradually, as the leading ships of the British line showed a most unexpected turn of speed and crept inexorably nearer, suspicions began to rise aboard *Gneisenau* that their first lieutenant's eyesight had been, after all, better than was allowed. As the suspicions rose hope sank, and something like despair took its place : by midday the fact that they would soon be in action against British battle-cruisers was known to all, and when the midday meal was served a quarter of an hour later, it was consumed with rather less enthusiasm than were the sandwiches aboard *Inflexible*. One can sympathize with some of the married men who—according to a later report—thought that in view of the immense odds against their survival, a surrender should be negotiated.

As the meal finished, the dull booming of *Inflexible*'s opening salvoes came across the water, and bugle-call and drum beat to quarters.

From the bridge the scene was ominous. Brown cordite fumes were splodged against the black screen of the battle-cruisers' smoke—now obviously and dishearteningly nearer—while below the clouds the stems cut fiercely towards them and huge bow waves fell away on either side. Jets of orange flame would shoot out through the clouds, and after an agonizing wait mast-high columns of water would rise—apparently soundlessly—alongside the hapless *Leipzig*. As the columns crashed, a fog would form momentarily, spreading laterally as though to reach towards them—and as it evaporated, the scream of the hurtling shell would arrive to underline the differences between those that had been fired at the German ships at Coronel, and those which now lay stacked in the handing rooms of the battle-cruisers.

Then came the instructions to the light cruisers to try to escape and to *Gneisenau* to accept action : *Nürnberg* broke away easily from the starboard side but *Dresden* was on the port bow and came sharply across *Gneisenau*'s bows, forcing the bigger ship to veer across her wake—a manœuvre which under different circumstances would surely have earned the light cruiser's captain a stinging rebuke. However, as the light cruisers bore away to the south and Captain Maerker settled his ship on her new course, the ranges closed and *Invincible*'s salvoes crashed into the sea ahead and alongside—and as *Gneisenau* steamed through the cascading waters, she was hit for the first time by a shell which tore away part of the outer casing of the third funnel and burst on the upper deck above the after starboard 8.2-inch casemate.

It was a foretaste of what was to come, for its splinters ripped downwards through two decks and buried themselves in a bunker, killing a stoker and tearing the forearms from a petty officer on their vicious way. By now the whole ship was a pulsating, echoing cavern of steel. Ammunition-trolleys rumbled across the wellrooms, the hoists whined up and down, transmitters shrieked and crackled and speaking-tubes blew their incessant, impatient summons. Fans whirred and the engines churned in an ever-faster rhythm—and all aboard awaited longingly for the illusory protection of their own gunfire.

It came at 1.30 p.m., as the four 8.2-inch turret guns answered the British fire—and even as their comforting bellow died away, the whole ship quivered and jumped as a second 12-inch shell exploded on the main deck, wrecking the boats and a range-finder, and damaging the after control position. Once more jagged splinters ripped open the deck and tore through the compartments below.

From the spotting positions on *Gneisenau*'s masts the gunnery officers could see the German salvoes falling just short of the cloud of smoke which hid all except the stem of the *Invincible* and the masts of both battle-cruisers, but when the range closed slightly and the cloud covered the whole area of the fall of shot, they had no means of telling whether their shells were hitting the targets or falling just short or over. The battle-cruisers' smoke was proving almost as great a nuisance to them as it was to Verner and his associates.

Then *Scharnhorst* surged up alongside to take the lead (showing already a ragged gash in her near side where a shell had obviously exploded between decks) and as she passed, both ships fired full salvoes from the turret guns, filling the hearts of all aboard with hope, for surely such thundering power could not fail to protect them. As though in confirmation, white clouds blossomed on *Invincible*'s foredeck and an orange flame glowed for a few seconds somewhere below her foremast.

Then water spouted high around *Scharnhorst*, a huge red flame burst from her quarterdeck and as she shuddered back on to an even keel, *Inflexible*'s salvoes plunged just short of *Gneisenau* herself, and a dull thud aft told of an underwater hit.

But the German ships were soundly built, and the British gunners during this first stage of the battle were still groping for their targets. There were no more hits on *Gneisenau* for the time being, and when von Spee took advantage of the wind, the smoke and the opening ranges to make his escape bid, she had only been hit three times. During the three-quarters of an hour which elapsed between the sharp turn southwards and the opening of the second phase of the engagement much of the damage was repaired. The littered chaos of cabins, gun-room and wardroom below the main deck was tidied up, instruments replaced in the control-room, a 22-pounder magazine which was flooding through the underwater hit was sealed off and a leak-stopper securely jammed into position. By 2.45 p.m., when the battle-cruisers re-opened fire after the chase to the southward, *Gneisenau* and her crew had made a sound recovery from their baptism of heavy fire.

For the moment von Spee held to his southerly course, waiting until the range had closed sufficiently for the German 8.2 casemate guns to be brought into action, then once again he took his two armoured cruisers around to the east to accept battle, and as *Gneisenau* steadied on her new course the heavy guns on both sides thundered in dreadful concert. *Scharnhorst* ahead was almost immediately blanketed from sight by huge waterspouts, which were still crashing back into the sea when *Gneisenau* reached the area; then more arose as *Inflexible*'s shells plummeted on and around her.

Almost immediately two shells landed between the second and third funnels, the first bursting in the men's galley-deck, scattering cooking-pots and saucepans like grapeshot, wrecking the port order-transmitting station and killing two men in the after 8.2-inch casemate. The second exploded on the armour of the upper deck and one of its splinters cut through a steam pipe. As stretcher-bearers and repair-parties went into action, smoke and gas billowed from a 6-inch shell-room where a ventilator shaft had been wrecked, and other splinters ripped through the casemate decks.

But as men in the port casemates were cut down, their places were taken by those from the 22-pounder batteries for it was obvious that these guns would not fire today. Another shell crashed down through the decks, bursting the steel walls of the food-store apart, its splinters plunging on down in a cone of destruction to bury themselves in the bunkers below. Another was deflected from its course and ploughed through cabins and messdecks leaving a trail of torn blankets, bunks and limbs : Lieutenant-Commander Verner and his guns-crews were growing more proficient.

Fire alarms jangled up forward on *Gneisenau* and as hosepipes uncoiled behind racing black-faced fire-parties, another shell burst below the main deck—and pipes and men were cut to ribbons. But *Gneisenau*'s guns still answered the British fire, and as yet the ammunition came regularly through the growing chaos of the decks. There were over seven hundred men aboard her and the ship could still be fought.

From the spotting position on the foremast the scene was still the same : the cloudless sky, the ruffled water, the huge cloud of smoke away to the north, punctured by golden jets and underlined by a foaming wake—while ahead the flagship still plunged onwards through a forest of waterspouts, her guns still firing regularly. But now long open gashes showed in her steel sides, through which the red-orange glow of fire could occasionally be seen. It seemed moreover to those who watched that *Scharnhorst* was lower in the water—and at about this time Captain Maerker noticed that one of her flags was flying at half-mast. As in the event of the death of von Spee, Captain Maerker, who was senior to Captain Schultze of the *Scharnhorst*, would assume command of the squadron, the following exchange of signals now took place :

Gneisenau to *Scharnhorst* : Why is the Admiral's flag at half-mast? Is the Admiral dead?
Admiral to Captain Maerker : No. I am all right so far. Have you hit anything?
Captain Maerker to Admiral : The smoke prevents all observation.
Admiral to Captain Maerker : You were right, after all.

One feels that this is an admission few men would have had the grace to make in the circumstances in which von Spee now found himself. The action between the heavy ships of both squadrons had by now been in progress for an hour and three-quarters, and the situation of his armoured cruisers was sufficiently similar to that of *Good Hope* and *Monmouth* at Coronel, for the conclusion to form in the minds of many of his officers and men that their fate would also coincide. It seems likely that there was also a determination to meet that fate in such a way that no odious comparisons could be drawn.

Like Cradock at Coronel, von Spee's tactics at this time were to endeavour imperceptibly to close the range until his secondary armament could be brought into action. Only in this way could the German broadside weight of fire hope to exact any payment at all for the havoc which was being wreaked by the British 12-inch shells—and for the moment it seemed that Admiral Sturdee was prepared to allow this closure of the range to take place. Gradually the two battle-lines drew nearer until the German port 5.9-inch batteries could reach the target at extreme elevation—but at this distance accuracy was impossible for such light armament, and in the meantime *Scharnhorst* and *Gneisenau* were paying too heavily for what was to prove in fact an almost negligible advantage. The flagship in particular came under dreadful fire from *Invincible*, whose gunnery officer had from the first enjoyed a clear picture of his target and had now settled down to a machine-like regularity and accuracy. Time after time, *Scharnhorst* lurched and juddered away to starboard as the heavy shells smashed their way down through the decks and exploded with devastating violence in mess-decks and casemates. From *Gneisenau*'s decks she could be seen to be burning fiercely in half a dozen places, and at about this time one of her 5.9-inch guns on the disengaged side was hit by a shell which dropped through the main deck and galley above, and exploded, tumbling gun, crew and housing out through the side of the ship.

But von Spee tried to lead even nearer—for in this course still lay the only hope his ships had of material justification for their sacrifice. It thus seems a little unfair that when Sturdee did eventually turn away, it was far more because of the smoke nuisance than of possible danger from enemy fire. Just before he did so (at 3.20 p.m., making the eighteen point turn which took the battle-cruisers back across their own wakes with *Inflexible* in the lead), *Scharnhorst*'s third funnel was shot away and a fire blazed fiercely on her foredeck.

Gneisenau too, was suffering under the salvoes which Lieutenant-Commander Verner had, with growing confidence and accuracy, directed upon her. Fires were raging between decks fore and aft, she had been badly holed below water alongside Number Three boiler-room, and as the pumps had no effect whatsoever the whole compartment had to be abandoned. As it filled, *Gneisenau* listed—and even as orders were given to flood the port compartment opposite, the steel plating to the starboard engine room was burst open and a dreadful explosion occurred inside which shook the ship from truck to keelson. Tons of water flooded in and cooled in death the agony of those caught in jets of steam and lakes of fire.

Now, while the turn away out of range by the battle-cruisers took place, the efforts of repair parties and stretcher-bearers could for a little while keep pace with the demands made upon them. Fires were brought under control, debris cleared from the wrecked and littered decks and flung overboard, tangled gear cut loose, the dead laid away in the forge. In the main dressing station surgeon and chaplain worked among the grim human wreckage of a naval action, and for the first time could be seen the effect of the explosion of lyddite shell on living flesh and blood. Men had been brought in unconscious and naked, their clothing stripped from them by blast from a shell bursting yards away and in an entirely different part of the ship. Some came in with limbs torn away by air pressure alone, others with not a mark on their bodies but their lungs paralysed or burst, or with the surface of their bodies whipped raw or burnt by blast—and they lay in serried rows between the blood-soaked blankets of those cut down by flying steel. And after the hits in boiler and engine-room, stretcher-bearers brought in stokers caught in pockets of scalding steam.

The relief occasioned by the battle-cruisers' turn did not last long. At 3.25 p.m. *Inflexible* came around, leading the line and clear of the flagship's smoke at last, to open fire again. As *Gneisenau* jumped and shook under more hits, von Spee in turn led the *Scharnhorst* around to double back and stop the British securing the lee position. As she went past *Gneisenau* the flagship could be seen from the spotting positions to be burning fiercely between decks and now to be about three feet lower in the water. Huge rents gaped in her plating and steam wreathed her quarterdeck, yet when her starboard batteries were engaged, their salvoes rang out as briskly and defiantly as ever.

Gneisenau followed *Scharnhorst* around and as she did so the British ships momentarily changed targets and *Gneisenau* came under fire from *Invincible*. The first shells crashed into the sea just short and drove the sea in torrents through the holes in her plating and across the shambles of her upper deck : fire parties found themselves temporarily unemployed but struggling to keep their feet in the surging flood, while stretcher-bearers lost their precious burdens and saw them swept overboard. Then the ship came around, the starboard batteries joined action for the first time and owing to *Scharnhorst*'s smoke, *Gneisenau* was lost to sight from the British decks. Although her fire was added to that of the flagship, for the moment she received none in return.

Instead of suffering physically themselves, those above decks could now watch the final annihilation of their sister-ship, with her complement and Admiral—realizing as they did so that in the very near future they too would face the same ordeal.

It must have been a shattering experience.

Under accurate and sustained fire from the two immensely more powerful battle-cruisers, *Scharnhorst* gradually lost shape and semblance of a fighting ship. The seas erupted about her, her funnels tipped awry, her upper decks disintegrated under the constant pounding, smoke belched from half a dozen fires within and her after-turret was reduced to nothing but a blazing cauldron. Yet despite all this her starboard batteries fired almost until the end—slowly and irregularly, but defiantly and as far as could be seen, accurately. Minute after endless minute ticked by, shell after shell crashed down into her, ragged salvo after ragged salvo flared from her casemates and forward turret—and inch by inch her stem cut lower into the shell-torn sea.

Then at 3.57 p.m., after enduring the pulverizing fire of both battle-cruisers for over twenty minutes, she ceased fire—possibly because ammunition for her remaining guns was no longer available. Slowly and painfully her bows went around until she was heading towards the enemy, and as she steadied on the new course von Spee sent his last signal to the *Gneisenau*. It read: 'Endeavour to escape if your engines are still intact'. With this humane if not exactly inspiring valediction, Graf von Spee took his flagship and all her company towards extinction.

Had he sailed under the White Ensign, his story would now be a part of a great tradition. As it is his name is more remembered today for a scuttled battleship in Montevideo Bay, and her captain's suicide in Buenos Aires.

It seems unlikely that anyone aboard *Gneisenau* actually witnessed the death of the flagship, for by that time she was heavily engaged herself. As has been related, she came clear of *Scharnhorst*'s smoke with her starboard batteries firing rapid and controlled salvoes at *Inflexible*, who immediately answered her, leaving *Invincible* to carry out Admiral Sturdee's intentions with regard to the *Scharnhorst*.

Gneisenau's speed by this time had been reduced to less than sixteen knots, and almost immediately one of *Inflexible*'s shells smashed into her foremost funnel, splitting the casing and bending the top half over almost horizontally. There was thus no chance whatsoever of her taking advantage of Graf von Spee's last instruction, and Captain Maerker was faced with a choice of surrender or annihilation. It does not appear that he wasted much thought on the former course of action, for he held his ship steadily to a course converging with that of *Inflexible*, and ordered stokers from the wrecked engine and boiler-rooms to augment the ammunition parties feeding the starboard batteries. Almost immediately *Inflexible* turned away again—a move designed in fact to abate the ever-present smoke nuisance, but one which probably had a tonic effect upon the German gun-crews, who can hardly be blamed in the circumstances for assuming that their own fire had been responsible. Their hearts rose.

But if the situation at this moment on the gun-decks was tolerable, that below decks resembled Dante's Inferno with some of the horrors of the Flood added. The starboard engine-room, the after boiler-room and the starboard after dynamo-room were now full of water through enemy action, and complementary compartments on the port side were flooded to reduce the list—and above the swirl and suck of enclosed water came the dreadful cries of trapped and drowning men, and the insistent jangle of the fire alarm. Yet no one could see the fire for the dense clouds of smoke, gas and coal dust which filled the after part of the ship below the armoured deck. Fire-parties and stretcher-bearers groped helplessly in utter darkness on their errands of repair or mercy until they were either beaten back by the choking fumes, or themselves lost and drowned or gassed in the black, sulphurous trap.

Then the shattered casing of the top half of the foremost tunnel fell away, the fans which were drawing in the poisonous fumes leaking from it were shut off, the atmosphere cleared somewhat, and coal dust settled in a thick scum on the imprisoned waters. It was then discovered that another shell from *Inflexible* had exploded in the bunker of Number Four boiler-room, reducing the coal to dust and driving it with the force of a sandstorm out into the adjacent compartments. As *Inflexible* was still completing her turn away, there was another slight pause in the action during which some of the confusion below was reduced. Then *Inflexible* was seen heading back as though to cross *Gneisenau*'s wake, and men were sent back to the port batteries to prepare for the expected onslaught when the battle-cruiser's move was complete.

As it happened *Inflexible* never did cross *Gneisenau*'s wake and secure the lee position, for by now *Invincible* had rejoined and Admiral Sturdee ordered a re-formation of the battle-line with the flagship again leading—much to Lieutenant-Commander Verner's disgust, for once more he found himself completely blinded by *Invincible*'s smoke. *Carnarvon* had at last arrived within range, coming up astern of the German cruiser and opening fire with her fore 7.5-inch guns.

It was by now 4.30 p.m., clouds obscured part of the sky and a light drizzle was falling—and *Gneisenau* began her single-handed battle against three enemy ships, two of which were each considered amply powerful enough to annihilate her without help.

During the first ten minutes of this action it seems as though the British gunnery was again finding difficulty in adjustment to alterations of course and position—and during the time they took to re-establish what Verner described as a 'grip on the target', *Gneisenau* hit *Invincible* three times, once below water. But it was to no avail. Soon salvoes of 12-inch shell were screaming across at her from both battle-cruisers, while *Carnarvon*'s port batteries were adding their lighter metal to the forces of destruction.

Almost immediately the starboard ventilating fans were destroyed, and as a result pressure in Number Four boiler-room began to drop alarmingly. Engineer-Officer Meyer and two stokers rapidly improvised a branch-lead from the ventilators of Number Five boiler-room—but Peter was being robbed to pay Paul while a full effort was needed from both. *Gneisenau*'s speed dropped another two knots and she became even easier to hit. The starboard side of the afterbridge was ripped open by splinters from below and the remainder of the foremost funnel crashed overboard.

And now the cumulative effect of the punishment the ship had been taking during the last three hours began to make itself felt. The casualty list had been mounting steadily and there were now no more spare gun-crews from the disengaged batteries to fill the vacancies in the casemates. The strength of the ammunition-parties was dwindling, and the task for those who remained grew more and more difficult as passages became choked with debris and the very decks themselves disintegrated under the hammering. Shells smashed away the roofs of the starboard 8.2-inch casemates, the guns themselves were being put out of action one by one, after which the process was repeated with the 5.9-inch casemates underneath. A port 8.2-inch casemate suffered a like fate to that of the *Scharnhorst*'s 5.9-inch, as one of *Inflexible*'s shells crashed through the upper deck, burst in the casemate and blew gun, crew and side-plating out into the sea. Every lyddite shell which burst aboard started a fire which raged unchecked until short shots flung tons of water through the gaping holes in the plating to quench it.

Yet still, somehow, guns were repaired and manned to make some sort of answer to the British fire. It was irregular, slow—and now unsuccessful. Incredibly, *Gneisenau*'s outward appearance had not greatly changed at this stage despite her internal plight, and when at 4.45 p.m. *Inflexible*'s captain, Phillimore, weary of the enveloping cloud from the flagship's funnels and guns, abruptly turned fourteen points to port without orders and ran through the smoke cloud and out into the sunlight, *Gneisenau* lay some 11,000 yards away on the starboard beam, looking, according to Verner, much the same as ever. *Inflexible* turned back to starboard, and with a clear and slow-moving target well within range, opened upon it the most devastating fire of which she was capable. In view of the developing circumstances it was perhaps a kind act on the part of Fate that one of her first shells should now burst in the main dressing-station and put the great majority of the wounded out of their suffering.

Of the situation aboard *Gneisenau* at this time, her executive officer, Commander Hans Pochhammer, was later to write :

> The ship had lost speed rapidly owing to damage in boilers and engine-room. Our guns also sustained further severe damage. A 12-inch shell broke through the deck of the starboard fore 8.2-inch casemate just above the bridge and killed the whole crew, Lieutenant Aneker in command of the battery and Lieutenant Pfulf, who was close to, escaped. The hit also took effect in the port 8.2-inch casemate and all the gun-crew except two men were put out of action.

Lieutenant Aneker it seemed, bore a charmed life, for he immediately took command of another casemate gun which five minutes afterwards suffered exactly the same fate as the one described by Pochhammer, and he then served as a member of a crew working a 5.9-inch gun. When this in turn was put out of action and all the crew except himself killed, he occupied himself carrying wounded to one of the improvised dressing-stations.

At this time another shortage became acute—that of battle-ensigns. Masts and jury-masts had been shot away so often that at one time no flags were flying at all, and as it happened this state of affairs coincided with a shortage of ammunition due to the jamming of one of the hoists. Not unnaturally, Captain Phillimore of *Inflexible* concluded that *Gneisenau* had struck, and he informed Admiral Sturdee of the fact. The British ships ceased fire and began to turn inwards, but the hoist came free and ammunition again reached the fore-turret which immediately fired a single shot at *Invincible*. The battle-cruisers swung away and once again the destruction was taken up.

The carnage and devastation wrought aboard *Gneisenau* now beggars description. Between the masts her decks were beaten away down to the armoured deck, and soon this too was torn open by the plummeting shells. Her after-turret was jammed at ninety degrees, all the starboard casemate guns were blown into the sea or pounded into shapeless masses of steel. Half her crew were dead or wounded, and now the wreck of the main dressing-station was repeated in the stokers' bathroom in which stretcher-bearers had been endeavouring to improvise a sick bay with what medical equipment and supplies remained. Now indeed, *Gneisenau* showed her wounds, and by 5.15 p.m. little remained of her but a reeking, blood-strewn hulk—and once again the British ships ceased fire.

One of *Carnarvon*'s last shots however, had buckled up *Gneisenau*'s armoured deck until it jammed against the steering-gear in the after torpedo-flat. As a result, *Gneisenau* turned slowly to starboard and by the time the gear was cleared she was practically doubling in her tracks—and it was found that the remaining guns on the port side could be brought to bear. They fired all except the last round of *Gneisenau*'s ammunition—and the salvoes which the battle-cruisers fired in reply at last finished her as a fighting ship. All her engine-rooms and boiler-rooms went out of action, the remaining casemate guns were silenced, and by 5.20 p.m. she was virtually stopped, listing so badly that water was flooding inboard through the lower starboard gun-ports.

Once more the British ships ceased fire—and less than a minute afterwards, an 8.2-inch shell was either found in the debris, or carried across the yawning chaos of the decks from the jammed after-turret to the empty handing-rooms of the fore-turret. Sometime about 5.30 p.m., *Gneisenau*'s last shot was fired. According to Verner it passed close above the heads of members of Y turret's gun-crews who had come up to watch the last minutes of the German cruiser's life, '. . . creating keen competition among them to return to their action stations', from which positions they once more opened fire, as did *Invincible*'s gun-crews.

Gneisenau's forecastle was blotted out, the turret severed from its trunk and hurled bodily overboard : now *Gneisenau* was at last completely without fighting power. In the shambles of the control-room, Captain Maerker listened to the reports coming in. There was no more ammunition—and the guns to fire it were wrecked anyway. His ship was stationary because there was no steam in the boilers, and slowly sinking because the pumps were out of action. Of his ship's complement over a half at least were dead, and many of the remainder were badly wounded. It thus seems that there was not one single thing he could do to continue the fight, for the British ships showed not the slightest inclination to come within range of his torpedoes, and the days when the end of a warship was fought out by close hand-to-hand combat across her decks were long past.

The only thing left for him to do was to make sure that nothing of value would fall into the enemy's hands—and it says much for the confidence of *Gneisenau*'s designers in the virtual unsinkability of their creation, that they had foreseen Captain Maerker's predicament at this moment and taken steps to aid him in it. Explosive charges were carried in special compartments between the inner and outer skins of *Gneisenau*'s hull, and at 5.40 p.m. Maerker gave the orders to prepare to sink the ship.

All survivors other than those actually to be engaged in this last task were ordered on deck, and hammocks and any other items of equipment likely to float were issued to them : Engineer-Officer Meyer estimated that there were about three hundred men left alive aboard the ship at this time.

When all was reported clear below, the order to blow up the ship was given and Engineer Lieutenant-Commander Thone fired the charges in the main engine-room while Sub-Lieutenant Proschwitzky did the same in the starboard engine-room—and either deliberately or accidentally lost his life while doing so, for he was never seen again. At the same time, the stern torpedoes were fired and the sluices left open to flood the compartments.

Gneisenau shook and seemed fractionally to right herself. Then she lay over about ten degrees to starboard and began slowly to settle. Captain Maerker called for three cheers for the Kaiser, and as the ragged, hoarse, but still defiant shouts died away, the men began to clamber across the decks and drop down into the ruffling, icy waters alongside. Captain Maerker, Commander Pochhammer and Engineer-Officer Meyer were all on the bridge at this time, and the latter's description of the events which followed is given in Captain (later Admiral) Raeder's *Cruiser Warfare*.

The Captain called for three cheers for the Kaiser and the ship was then abandoned. I slipped down from the bridge on the port side and fell into the water on the starboard side, the ship having suddenly capsized. When I came to the surface, I saw the fore-part of the ship rise up again, keel uppermost, about thirty yards away.

There were four men sitting on the torpedo-tube, waving and singing, and presently the ship disappeared for the last time, carrying them down with her. Men clinging to floating objects around me were singing 'The Song of the Flag' and other patriotic songs. One man gave three cheers for the sunken ship and the cheers were taken up repeatedly by others. . . . The temperature of the water was only 39 deg. Fahrenheit and during the half hour's immersion, many of my companions perished. I and twelve others were clinging to a hammock and a round beam of wood about twelve inches thick and fourteen feet long, and we were all picked up by the *Inflexible*. I was amazed at the spirit displayed by the men and made the discovery that descriptions of the kind that I had read were not merely literary adornment invented by the authors.

When *Gneisenau* went down, the battle-cruisers were some three to four thousand yards away and they closed in towards the groups of survivors, carrying out hasty repairs on their boats as they did so, for shell-splinters had inevitably torn through the wooden skins to render them temporarily unseaworthy. *Inflexible* got two boats away, as did *Carnarvon*, but quite a number of the German survivors actually reached the sides of the ships and either climbed up themselves or were hauled up by ropes. Some achieved the half-mile swim but were then so weakened by shock and their own exertions, that they failed to grip the trailing ropes and sank tragically beneath the eyes of their would-be rescuers.

It seems that Captain Maerker was not picked up, although at one time it was thought that he had been. *Gneisenau*'s commander —Corvetten-Kapiten Pochhammer—was found by one of *Inflexible*'s boats, and was so exhausted that he had to be lifted inboard, but the indestructible Lieutenant Aneker arrived safely aboard the *Carnarvon*, as did another young officer who announced as he drank his cocoa : 'I believe I have a cousin in one of the British ships. His name is Stoddart.'

The Admiral's surprise was as great as his own.

In all, one hundred and eighty-seven of *Gneisenau*'s crew were saved, including seventeen officers. Once they had recovered from the immediate effects of the action, they all showed a tendency to talk about their experiences and they were obviously heartened by any words of praise for their recent fight which were offered, but after about half an hour of loquacity, they relapsed into an exhausted, rather apathetic silence. Soon most of them were asleep, and a few did not wake again.

That evening, a message arrived aboard *Inflexible* from Admiral Sturdee. It read :

Please convey to Commander of Gneisenau.
The C.-in-C. is very gratified that your life has been spared and we all feel that *Gneisenau* fought in a most plucky manner to the end. We much admire the good gunnery of both ships, we sympathize with you in the loss of your Admiral and so many officers and men. Unfortunately the two countries are at war, the officers of both Navies who can count friends in the other have to carry out their country's duty, which your Admiral, Captain and Officers worthily maintained to the end.

A verdict, one feels, which has withstood the test of time.

CHAPTER TEN

THE battle of the giants was thus virtually over by 6 p.m. That of the smaller ships was not, although one was fast reaching its climax.

When the German light cruisers broke away in response to von Spee's signal to endeavour to escape, some ten miles separated them from the British ships which were to pursue them. *Leipzig* and *Nürnberg*, being respectively astern and to starboard of the armoured cruisers, swung away to the southward with no trouble or delay. So, in fact, did *Dresden*—despite her position ahead and to port of *Gneisenau*, for she passed the trouble and inconvenience of her move on to the bigger ship, and then pelted away to the southward as hard as she could go. As she was a younger ship than either of her two consorts, and as her engines were in considerably better shape than theirs, she was soon well ahead; of the five other ships on both sides, only *Glasgow*—thoroughly overhauled at Rio only a few weeks before—possessed comparable steaming powers.

Ten miles behind, *Kent* and *Cornwall* had swung away from the battle-cruisers in similar manœuvres to those of *Leipzig* and *Nürnberg* while *Glasgow*, with rather more regard for naval propriety than *Dresden* had shown, doubled back and came around under *Inflexible*'s stern. She thus lost ground and began the chase some eleven miles behind *Leipzig* and *Nürnberg*, and at least twelve behind *Dresden*—the enemy whom only *Glasgow* possessed the speed to catch.

The ensuing hour showed clearly the differing steaming abilities of the various ships. At the beginning, the British line from west to east was *Cornwall, Kent* and *Glasgow* (astern), and they chased to the south-east a similarly disposed German line in the order *Leipzig, Nürnberg* and *Dresden*. By the end of the hour however, both *Glasgow* and *Dresden* had overtaken their consorts and crossed in front of them—*Dresden* fleeing due southwards and *Glasgow* chasing her—*Kent* and *Cornwall* were keeping together, but poor *Leipzig* was once more dropping behind.

From the point of view of anyone who knew the British ships but was not present at the time, it would have seemed an obvious move to have allocated the lame duck of the German squadron—*Leipzig*—to the lame duck of the County class cruisers—and she, it had been accepted for years, was undoubtedly *Kent*. But extraordinary things were happening inside the engine and boiler-rooms of Captain Allen's command; in response to the needs of the moment and in accordance with the atmosphere of intense excitement and exhilaration which reigned on board, the sweating, half-naked stokers were forcing the boiler-pressures up to unprecedented heights, and for the moment at any rate the boilers took the strain. The hands of the revolution-counters crept further and further around the dials.

This may have been due partly to the fact that the ship was light, for she had steamed down from Abrolhos and had not even commenced coaling when *Nürnberg* and *Gneisenau* had appeared over the horizon. But every advantage has to be paid for somehow, and there was an obvious drawback about engaging in a long stern chase with virtually empty bunkers. The wardroom furniture was the first combustible material to augment the exiguous coal-supply, and in due course, mess-tables, benches, the chaplain's lectern and the paymaster's desk all followed one another into the flames. By the end, deck timbers were being ripped up to feed the ravenous furnaces.

By four o'clock *Kent* was racing through the seas at the unprecedented speed of twenty-four knots, and by this time it was quite obvious that she and *Cornwall* were fast overtaking *Leipzig*, and slowly gaining on *Nürnberg* as well. *Leipzig* was to starboard of *Nürnberg*, *Cornwall* was level with and to starboard of *Kent*—and to take diagonally opposite targets would have lost hardly-won time for the British ships; to arrange matters, therefore, signals passed between the two captains and as a result *Kent* and her crew settled down to the task of removing for ever from her reputation the stigma of poor steaming. She altered course very slightly to port, and was very soon inexorably creeping up on *Nürnberg*.

Nevertheless, her first shots were fired at *Leipzig*. By 4.15 p.m., *Kent* was slightly ahead of *Cornwall*, and as it seemed that *Leipzig* might possibly now be just within range of her foremost guns, the opportunity was too good to be missed. Salvoes were fired from *Kent*'s twin 6-inch turret and the fore starboard 6-inch casemate, and for some twenty seconds after the guns had fired hardly a word other than routine command was spoken. Then as waterspouts rose well short of the target, *Leipzig*'s stern-most guns and port after battery answered, and in due course the German 4.1-inch shells plummeted into the water. They did so almost alongside *Kent*—and this demonstration of the difference in ranges between German and British guns was sobering—but not depressing.

Then almost as though the shots had been a pre-arranged signal, *Nürnberg* altered course two points to port and bore off to the eastward—a move which enabled *Kent* to cut the slight corner as she altered on to a converging course.

As the afternoon had passed, the sky had clouded over. Now, as *Kent* left *Glasgow*, *Cornwall* and *Leipzig* away to the starboard, mist began to form and the visibility dropped. Excitement therefore gave way to some anxiety, for although it was evident that *Kent* was gaining on *Nürnberg*, it was at a snail's pace and time was now on the German's side. Already it was only just possible to see the enemy light cruiser without high-powered glasses, and if the mist thickened any more, *Nürnberg* might well pass out of sight and make good her escape. By 4.45 p.m. *Kent* was steaming at twenty-five knots and had cut *Nürnberg*'s lead down considerably, but the vibration aboard was so great that the range-finders

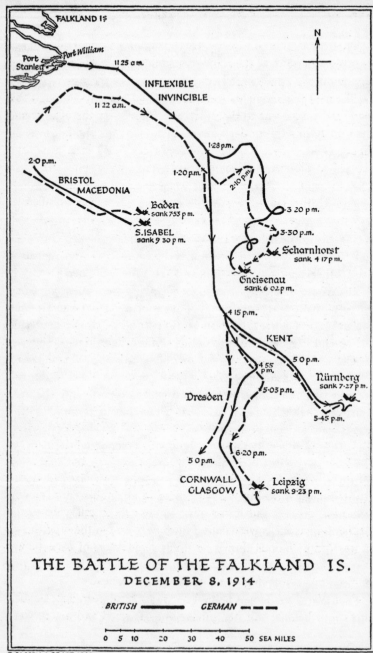

THE BATTLE OF THE FALKLAND IS.
DECEMBER 8, 1914

BRITISH —————— GERMAN — — — —

0 5 10 20 30 40 50 SEA MILES

© CASSELL & CO. LTD. 1960.

were useless. The mist was thickening and a slight drizzle began.

Then at 5.00 p.m., by which time *Nürnberg* had led imperceptibly around until the course was south-east again, the German ship suddenly opened fire with her stern 4.1-inch guns.

The next few moments were not without comedy—though this was hardly apparent to those present. Frantically the officers and men on *Kent*'s upper deck searched the seas for the fall of shot. Another salvo flared from *Nürnberg*'s stern 4·1-inch guns and seemed to disappear so completely that glasses scanned the horizons to see if by chance she was firing at some other ship. It was not until the third salvo was fired and fell just over *Kent*'s stern, that it was realized aboard the British ship that they were now well within range of *Nürnberg*'s guns and that her opening shots had passed high above them. But when *Kent* replied with her fore 6-inch turret guns at extreme elevation the water-spouts still rose disappointingly short.

The next twenty minutes must have been a period of extreme frustration for all members of both crews engaged in the battle. *Nürnberg* had the range perfectly and her guns fired with great precision and accuracy—but with no luck. *Kent* was straddled continuously, generally on each side of the forebridge, but she was only hit once—by a shell which burst on the upper deck aft, and did practically no damage at all.

Kent was firing from her fore-turret and her forward 6-inch casemate on the starboard side, and her shells fell into the water alternately to left and right of the target with monotonous and exasperating regularity. She was still gaining on *Nürnberg* it was true—but the visibility was worsening in an almost exactly compensating degree, and it was quite impossible to tell whether the British 6-inch shells were falling short or over. On the other hand, it was quite obvious that it was only a question of time before *Nürnberg*'s astonishingly near-misses became actual hits—and one or two lucky shots might still enable her to escape.

Poor *Nürnberg*. Hopes aboard her must have been kept in such precarious balance, for her gunnery was so good and her services to her country and admiral had been faithful and devoted. But at about 5.35 p.m., when the mist was thickening every minute and her chances of escape looked highest, two of her long overworked and now overpressed boilers burst, and her speed dropped catastrophically to nineteen knots. As *Kent* raced up on her port quarter, Captain von Schönberg took his little ship around for her last fight. It was just 5.45 p.m.

To the men of *Kent*, this was a great moment. As *Nürnberg* came around eight points to port, Captain Allen altered six points on to a converging course, the range closed abruptly to 6,000 yards, and with his ship steady on the *Nürnberg*'s port bow, independent fire from her starboard batteries was poured into the German cruiser. For a few moments the effect was not completely devastating, but then the order was given to change from firing common shell to lyddite, and at once the picture changed.

A fire blazed up almost immediately by *Nürnberg*'s mainmast, and soon afterwards her main-topmast fell gracefully forward. The casings of her funnels began to split apart as splinters from the exploding shells tore through them, reducing them to sieves and ripping away the rigging and aerials. Shell ploughed up the decks and burst violently above and in the casemates, wrecking the guns, picking up the crews like dolls and flinging them into the sea or smashing them against the straining bulkheads.

The clangour aboard both ships was hellish. Guns fired independently and therefore continuously, and the rare intervals between the fire was filled with the crash and explosion of enemy shell. On *Kent* this was bad enough, for *Nürnberg*'s gunnery was still good and her shells crashed time and time again against the armoured belt—but on the German ship senses were utterly numbed by the sheer enormity and violence of the din. Minute after dreadful minute passed and the horror and devastation continued; almost it might have been better for the men aboard if her magazines could have been fired as *Good Hope*'s had been, and their sufferings ended in one last overwhelming explosion.

But it was not to be. For nearly twenty minutes the broadside pounding continued, and as *Nürnberg*'s speed dropped and her fire at last began to slacken, *Kent* drew ahead on to her port bow and fired from the after-turret. Then at 6.02 p.m., as though seeking relief from incessant punishment, *Nürnberg*'s bows turned away to starboard. *Kent*, with her now much greater speed, swung around level with her, keeping up the fire and holding the broadside position. As *Nürnberg*'s fire fell away even more, Captain von Schönberg took the brave but surely fatal course of turning towards the enemy in an attempt to bring his as yet unused starboard batteries into action.

As he turned to port, *Kent* held her course—and 'crossed the enemy's T'. For a moment, all that could reply to *Kent*'s entire starboard broadside were *Nürnberg*'s two forward upper-deck guns —and before they had a chance to do so, two lyddite shells burst simultaneously on the forecastle and wrecked them both.

Nürnberg continued her slow and labouring turn : *Kent* steamed on and began to turn in on an opposite course to that of her enemy. But it was no part of Captain Allen's plan to expose his ship to the danger of *Nürnberg*'s stern torpedoes, and he had also just received a severe warning that his ship was not—even now—completely triumphant or the enemy completely beaten.

Not only was his ship's foretopgallantmast swinging uselessly in its stays as a result of a shot through the heel, but a shell had burst just outside the midship casemate with results which only narrowly escaped blowing his ship and all her company sky-high. Shell-splinters tore through the 6-inch casemate, killing one man instantly and starting a fire, fierce and sudden enough to cause severe burns to the other nine men in the casemate. Moreover the ammunition-hoist had been open and the flash passed down the hoist and ignited a charge which was hooked on at the bottom—in the ammunition passage.

It was indeed fortunate for *Kent* that at the bottom of the hoist was also Sergeant Charles Mayes of the Royal Marine Light Infantry. He tore the burning charge from the hook, slammed tight the sliding scuttle in the hoist and yelled to the men around to fetch hoses. He had isolated the fire from the magazine, but was still in possession of a burning cordite charge, and before the hoses arrived he had perforce to throw down the charge in a place where it would do least harm—not an easy place to find in a confined ammunition passage. By the time the hoses arrived, empty shell-bags were burning with the original charge inside, but Sergeant Mayes had isolated the cordite in the vicinity and soon everything was soaking wet and the flames out. But for safety's sake, the sergeant then very wisely flooded the entire compartment.

And in the conning-tower, Captain Allen gave orders to turn the *Kent* fourteen points to port, to take her back parallel with the *Nürnberg*'s course and at a greater range. Much to their joy, the gun-crews of the port battery now came into action for the first time.

By 6.18 p.m. the range had opened to nearly 5,000 yards and *Nürnberg* was again under heavy fire—but it was evident that she could not last much longer. By 6.25 p.m. she was virtually stopped, her upper works a smoking, tangled ruin and her forepart wreathed in flames. When, eleven minutes later, her desultory fire at last ceased completely, *Kent*'s batteries followed suit and comparative silence fell upon the troubled scene.

Captain Allen took his ship around to starboard and then back across his own tracks until he faced towards the stricken enemy.

Nürnberg lay about five thousand five hunded yards away, burning fiercely—a complete wreck without a sign of life or movement except for her colours, which still fluttered at the peak. Slowly *Kent* approached, the range decreased and all aboard the British ship waited for the colours to come down. Captain Allen was now in a similar situation to that which had faced Captain von Schönberg when *Nürnberg* found *Monmouth* after the main action off Coronel—and doubtless his feelings were similar too.

But so was his duty. The flag still flew, *Nürnberg* showed no signs of sinking and her fires were abating, so at 6.45 p.m. *Kent* opened fire again and at 6.57 p.m. the colours came down—shot away or hauled down is still a matter of argument. But it was taken that the battle was at an end, so *Kent* ceased fire and approached, while her crew hastily patched up the splinter-torn boats in order to rescue what survivors there could be.

Months afterwards, one of those survivors, Chief Warrant Officer Rasch, was to write from memory the story of the last hour of *Nürnberg*'s life. Poor visibility and perhaps the fallibility of human memory account for the differences between the two pictures presented.

At about 6.30 p.m., Captain von Schönberg gave the order to blow up the ship.

The stokehold and engine-room personnel and all who had been on duty below came on deck and were ordered to get out the hammocks. As soon as they had provided themselves with some kind of floating object, they jumped overboard. After about thirty or forty had got away from the ship, *Kent* re-opened fire, her first rounds falling where the group of swimmers were thickest.

Lieutenant-Commander von Bülow, Dr Luedtke, Sub-Lieutenant Berndt, Warrant Officer Kohler and I sought protection behind No. 5 starboard gun. The flag at the peak having been shot away, Lieutenant-Commander von Bülow gave the order to hoist a new one, and Sub-Lieutenant Berndt accordingly hoisted a flag on the davit of the starboard after cutter, as there was no halyard on the mainmast.

When *Kent* had ceased fire, I saw the adjutant, Sub-Lieutenant Graf von Spee, go aft on the deck-house and with Lieutenant-Commander Kale, join the other officers. Captain von Schönberg was probably killed in the conning-tower by *Kent*'s final rounds.

Warrant Officer Kohler and some of the men lowered the first cutter filled with wounded—including Paymaster-Lieutenant Pichert. The cutter had hardly left the ship's side before it began to sink owing to damage which had not been observed. The surfboat was also lowered but capsized shortly afterwards with its occupants.

Lieutenant-Commander von Bülow and six other officers stood on the deckhouse together discussing how they could signal a request to *Kent* to dispatch a boat for the wounded.

Sub-Lieutenant von Spee fetched a pocket-lamp and signalled in Morse code. As it was still fairly light the signal was not observed.

Lieutenant-Commander von Bülow ordered all the port-holes between decks to be opened so that the ship would sink more rapidly. She listed further and further to starboard and the wounded slipped from the deck into the water. Lieutenant-Commander von Bülow, standing on the rail above Number 4 starboard gun, without a coat and up to his ankles in water, called for three cheers for the Kaiser.

All around him was getting quieter, for most of those in the water had died of cold or were already some distance from the ship. *Nürnberg* herself had suffered severely. The foremast was shot away down to the searchlight position, the funnels were riddled like sieves, the bridge and charthouse and the whole forepart of the ship were in flames, and even the flag on the cutter-davit had been torn in half.

The railing around the deck-house was still three or four feet above water when the gunnery officer and Sub-Lieutenants Berndt and Schack jumped overboard, and when the water reached the deck light of the Captain's sitting-room, I too left the ship.

Nürnberg turned on to her starboard side at 7.27 p.m., and sank quietly without any explosion. As she went down a group of men was seen from the *Kent* to be standing on her stern, apparently singing or cheering. One of them was waving a long piece of wood and to it was lashed a German ensign—so whatever had occurred before, *Nürnberg*'s flag was flying at the end.

Kent's boats searched the area until dark, but only twelve survivors were found still alive, and of these five died from shock and wounds within a few hours.

Graf Otto von Spee had not enjoyed his inheritance for long.

When *Leipzig* replied to *Kent*'s fire at 4.15 p.m., she had already been exchanging occasional salvoes with *Glasgow* for the preceding hour and a half. To all aboard *Leipzig* it must have been fairly evident from the first that whatever the fate in store for the other ships of the Asiatic Squadron, she at any rate had virtually no hope of escape. Far too many months had gone by and far too much water had passed under her keel since her last refit, for her mechanical condition to be in anything but second class order—and whatever the speed of the armoured cruisers *Kent* and *Cornwall* astern of her, it was quite obvious that *Glasgow* at least had something like five knots superiority.

But there are compensations for every disadvantage and the six sea months which had exacted their toll from *Leipzig's* engines, had also welded her crew into a fighting unit of high efficiency and excellent morale. When at 2.53 p.m. *Glasgow's* Captain Luce decided to open fire on the *Leipzig* at 12,000 yards, the German ship immediately responded by wheeling to starboard to bring her whole battery into action, firing three salvoes in as many minutes (which straddled *Glasgow*, whereas the British shells fell short) and then, as Captain Luce prudently took his ship out of range, the German light cruiser resumed course with a series of movements as neat and exact as those of any Pomeranian Grenadier on parade.

But of course *Leipzig* had lost ground by this necessity to turn and fire, and the fact that *Kent* and *Cornwall* were now some thousand yards nearer their quarry as a result was not lost upon Captain Luce. Once more *Glasgow* crept nearer, once more her bow guns opened fire, once more *Leipzig* turned to starboard and neatly bracketed *Glasgow* between successive salvoes.

But it must be remembered that *Glasgow* too was manned by long-service officers and ratings. This time Captain Luce pressed in until the range was down to 9,500 yards and the British salvoes could straddle the German cruiser. They did more—they hit her. One of *Leipzig's* 4·1-inch guns on the starboard side was wrecked, two of the gun-crew were killed; forecastle linoleum and mats upon which ready ammunition was lying were set alight, and rigging was shot away; then one shell exploded in the upper after bunker, and the resultant air-pressure burst open the bunker hatches and hurled them high into the air. Most damaging of all, splinters ripped through the deck into a bunker in use, air-pressure escaped through the bunker and the hole in the deck, and the forced draught in boiler-rooms three and four fell. Until the hole was blocked with blankets and a tub of water, pressure in *Leipzig*'s boilers dropped steadily, and when at 3.30 p.m. *Glasgow* again drew out of range, it was obvious that *Kent* and *Cornwall* were creeping inexorably nearer to the German ship.

At this time, there must have been considerable speculation aboard *Leipzig* as to the course of action which the various ships on each side would follow. Three British ships chased three Germans : would this develop into three isolated single-ship actions, or would the slower German ships be expected to fight a delaying action with the enemy and so increase the already excellent chances of the fast-steaming *Dresden*? From a tactical point of view there could only be one answer, but the human mind must be trained to objectivity and there must have been some bitter thoughts aboard *Leipzig* when it was seen that *Dresden*—after only a token attempt to attract *Glasgow*'s attention away—bore further and ever further away to the southwards, while *Glasgow* herself reduced speed until she was steaming comfortably along on *Leipzig*'s quarter, and *Cornwall* and *Kent* drew closer and closer.

By four o'clock, *Leipzig* was again under fire and had indeed—though this was not realized at the time—received what was to prove a fatal injury. One of *Glasgow*'s shells had set fire to the clothes store, and before the presence of the conflagration had been completely appreciated, the flames were licking hungrily forward into the next compartment and securing a firm hold on the after part of the ship below the messdeck. As the wind was still from the starboard quarter however, the flames drew over to port, and the starboard after guns were still able to keep up a brisk fire. Lieutenant Johnke in the foretop enthusiastically (and correctly) reported hits on *Glasgow*'s funnels and masts and far more attention was paid to damage inflicted on the enemy than on *Leipzig*'s own internal condition.

Then at about 4.20 p.m. came a pause in the action. *Glasgow* was seen to draw back out of range again and alter course to pass astern of *Cornwall* thus enabling her to attack *Leipzig* from the same side as the armoured cruisers. *Cornwall* and *Kent* were only just creeping up within range and so for the moment the guns were silent.

It was during this pause that the full effect of the fire in the clothes store aboard *Leipzig* was first appreciated. Commander Kretschmer led the fire parties personally, and with smoke helmets on they managed to fight their way into the neighbouring compartment, only to be beaten back by the intense heat, for by a cruel stroke of fate, *Leipzig* had been hit in such a manner that the following—and now stiffening—breeze, blew in through one shell-hole and out threw another, fanning the flames to a devouring fury as it did so. It was completely impossible to get to the actual seat of the fire in the clothes store, and Commander Kretschmer decided that for the moment he must concentrate on preventing it from spreading—and was immediately faced with the kind of dilemma which chills the blood even when considering it from a distance.

One of the first and most obvious precautions for him to take to limit the fire, was to flood the forepart of Number Two compartment—but through this compartment lay the chief means of access and escape from the main steering compartment, in which one brother officer and ten men were stationed. There was an emergency escape route, it was true, but as that was out through the clothes store itself, the only alternative which it offered to the men beyond would be that of a possibly quicker, but infinitely more painful death. Commander Kretschmer did his duty and flooded the compartment—but he later begged the captain not to turn the ship head to wind to deliver a torpedo attack as this would have meant the certain and almost immediate cremation of the men aft. When the end came he was still trying to fight his way through the flames to rescue them.

By now *Cornwall* and *Kent* were within range and firing their forward 6-inch guns at *Leipzig*, who replied with three after guns on the starboard side and one on the port side. Then *Nürnberg* swung off to the eastward with *Kent* after her, thus affording

Leipzig some relief, and the worsening weather raised hopes throughout the German squadron. For *Leipzig*, the presence of rain clouds seemed to hold the greatest degree of hope, both to dowse her fires and to cloak her movements, but this indeed was a day of misfortunes for German sailors, for when raindrops did patter on the decks and hiss in the inferno below, they were always accompanied by fierce gusts of wind which fanned the flames far more than the rain quenched them.

Then the Chief Engineer-Officer reported to the captain that pressure must be eased off or the boilers would burst—and so, faced by the same circumstances as his Admiral and his brother captains on *Gneisenau* and *Nürnberg*, Captain Haun took his ship slightly around to starboard to present a full broadside to his powerful opponents, and to fight it out to the end.

By now *Cornwall* had established the range and her 6-inch salvoes crashed on and around *Leipzig* with relentless regularity. The remainder of the rigging and the main and auxiliary aerials were shot away (which at least released wireless and signal personnel for the more urgent business of transporting ammunition). The superstructure began to disintegrate and jagged holes appeared in the decks, through which licked the tongues of flame from the holocaust below. The foretopmast went by the board and the gunnery lieutenant was killed; another shell started a fire in the forecastle and others penetrated upper and cross-bunkers until Number Four boiler-room was flooded and *Leipzig*'s speed dropped still lower—and all the time, amid the crash of her own guns and the sickening jar and explosion of enemy shell between her decks, the toll in dead and dying steadily mounted.

By five o'clock, all internal communication systems had been destroyed and the noise of battle was so tremendous that no one could make himself heard above it. Officers made their way around the decks on tours of inspection, encouraging the men by signs, jumping the yawning and often flame-filled chasms, clambering blackened and twisted ladders, forcing their way through passages blocked with debris and choked with smoke. They returned to the bridge, scorched, blistered and bloodstained, and shouted their reports into their captain's ear or indicated their findings by tragic pantomime.

By six o'clock the ammunition for the after guns was almost exhausted, only two hundred rounds remained forward and these had not yet been fused—but the ship was moving through the water and could still be fought. Then as orders were given for the remaining ammunition to be carried aft, another factor was brought into play against the German ship. Visibility was declining and Captain Luce ordered *Cornwall* to close and change from firing common shell to lyddite. The effect was immediate, and as devastating as it had been in the other actions fought this day. From a range of just over seven thousand yards, *Cornwall* fired salvo after salvo into the doomed vessel, every salvo hitting and every shell exploding; *Leipzig* was inexorably reduced to the flaming core of a mass of black, billowing smoke.

Yet still she managed to fire her remaining guns. Ammunition was transported aft to the batteries in action, by officers whose gun-crews had been killed or whose guns were wrecked or unable to bear; by the navigating officer whose charts and instruments were now but charred linen and twisted metal; by the signals officer whose entire department had been reduced to chaos—and in the lee of the bulkhead which separated that chaos from the shambles of the main deck, his few remaining hands fused the last shells aboard *Leipzig*, directed and assisted by the Ordnance Warrant Officer.

By seven o'clock they had all been fired. Not one round of ammunition remained, and in any case by now only the forward guns on the port side were undamaged and they could not be brought to bear. On receiving the surviving gunnery officer's report, Captain Haun turned to the torpedo officer and said 'Go ahead. It's your turn now', and with commendable attention to duty but not the remotest chance of success the starboard tube was cleared, and between 7.15 p.m. and 7.20 p.m. three torpedoes were fired.

But to no avail, for the two British ships were not to be enticed within torpedo range while *Leipzig*'s flag still flew, and at 7.20

p.m., having exhausted every possible means of inflicting damage upon his opponents, Captain Haun ordered the *Leipzig* to be sunk. The same measures which had been taken by men aboard two ships of the Imperial German Navy during the preceding hours were now repeated on a third. Seacocks were opened, condenser doors removed, torpedo tubes opened.

Gradually the survivors abandoned their stations and wearily made their way up to the after part of the forecastle, practically the only part of the upper deck neither wreathed in flames nor buried beneath piles of tangled wreckage and broken bodies. There were many wounded, and the exposed flesh and clothing of practically everybody was stained bright yellow by fumes from the explosions of lyddite. Commander Kretschmer and his fire parties were no longer in action, for most of them were dead and the rest were aiding the wounded. Thus the fires fore and aft raged unchecked, huge flames burst upwards through the quarterdeck sending showers of sparks out across the tumbling seas, transforming the after part of the ship into a torch, licking the base of the mainmast into a white, incandescent sheath of metal which eventually buckled as the ship heeled over to port and the whole mast toppled into the sea.

Amid the ruins of his ship, Captain Haun remained calm and imperturbable. He moved among the survivors, distributing cigarettes, talking quietly and cheerfully to them, encouraging the wounded, supervising the distribution of hammocks, buoys and the few remaining swimming-jackets. When it seemed that no living member of his crew was left below he called for three cheers for the Kaiser and while waiting for the British ships to close and take off the last survivors, he led them in singing 'The Song of the Flag'. It is said that he also gave permission for the flag to be lowered if anyone could reach it—but by now the flames clustered tight around the base of the foremast and the only man to try to reach the flag above, perished among them and the flag still flew.

Thus, to Captain Luce, *Leipzig* was still in action.

At 7.17 p.m. he had signalled by Morse code to the stricken ship that he was anxious to save life and asking if the *Leipzig* would surrender, but as at the time the German torpedo personnel were still endeavouring gallantly but vainly to strike their last dying blow against his ship, he had received no reply—if indeed, his signal was seen or understood.

He had then waited for nearly half an hour for some sign of reply to his signal, or of agreement with his suggestion—but it was his duty to safeguard his ship and the lives of the men aboard her. He therefore kept away from the bearings of *Leipzig*'s stern torpedo-tubes and at a distance of some three thousand yards from her. Visibility was falling, *Leipzig* was wreathed in flames and smoke and even through the most powerful binoculars it was impossible to perceive what was happening aboard her. It was clear that she was doomed, but it seemed to Captain Luce that she was still moving slowly forward, and he was by no means certain that the next explosion which occurred aboard her might not be that of a charge firing another round from a repaired gun.

Above all, her flag still flew, and while it flew Captain Haun would be acting within the accepted rules of naval warfare if he lured the British ships in close by a pretence of total defeat, only to open fire at point-blank range. Such a stratagem would not enable *Leipzig* to escape, but it would almost certainly take a toll of British lives, and might well impair *Glasgow*'s ability to find and sink the *Dresden*—a task which Captain Luce saw quite clearly could only be carried out *economically* by his ship.

And he can hardly be counted inhuman if at this moment he also remembered the seventy-five gun-flashes which echoed over the horizon off Coronel, and beat the death-knell of *Monmouth*. Whether or not this recollection played any part in deciding him upon his next action is not known, but it should be remembered that he was facing exactly the same basic situation as had Captain Allen of *Kent* already that evening, and Captain von Schönberg five weeks before.

At 7.50 p.m. he ordered his own guns and those aboard *Cornwall* to reopen fire—still firing lyddite shell.

153

The effect on the crowds of men gathered on *Leipzig*'s deck was horrific. Shell after shell burst violently among them, mowing down fifty or a hundred at the time, stripping limbs and heads from agonized trunks, splattering blood about the deck and the shambles of the superstructure as though with a giant paintbrush dipped in a slaughterer's trough. Men went mad with pain as their flesh was torn away from their bones and the heat from the explosions cauterized the open wounds. Blast picked bodies from the deck and tossed them high into the air, sometimes tearing them apart as they spun and twisted, sometimes dropping them whole and complete into the sea—icy beyond imagination after the pulsing furnace which *Leipzig* had become.

Men sought shelter behind the flimsy gun-shields only to be cut down by ricochetting splinters, or flying metal stripped from the remains of the superstructure. By the port cutter a group of men had been working repairing the boat, collecting the wounded and placing them in the bottom; two shells exploded almost simultaneously among them and here the slaughter was complete almost to the point of obliteration.

In the face of such appalling devastation many men chose the seemingly lesser risk of death by drowning and jumped overboard, but only the stoutest constitutions could stand the abrupt change in extreme temperatures and most of them died of the shock within a few seconds of hitting the water, their corpses rocking away on the lumpy sea, out of the circle of reflected fire and into the darkness beyond.

Then at last, by accident or design, two green flares burnt brilliantly on *Leipzig*'s quarterdeck—and Captain Luce decided to accept them as a signal of surrender. Aboard *Leipzig*, the violence and shock of explosion ceased and the pitiably few survivors of *Leipzig*'s once-proud crew staggered from their places of refuge to gather once more on the open deck by the conning-tower. There were only about twenty-four of them; twenty minutes before, there had been over two hundred. But Captain Haun was still alive and he once again instructed each man to secure for himself a hammock or lifebuoy.

By now it was raining, and away from the heat of the subsiding flames, extremely cold. It was also dark—and there was no sign of the enemy. *Leipzig* was a doomed hulk on an empty sea, and none it seemed, would watch her death or prevent a single member of her crew from dying with her. And after the events of the last hour there were some who stated that they preferred to die, than to live by the grace of an enemy who would fire on a defenceless ship.

Then just before nine o'clock a searchlight was suddenly switched on and it spelled out a message to the effect that boats were on their way to rescue those who remained. Soon afterwards, one of *Glasgow*'s cutters was seen slowly approaching, and when it was within a hundred yards Captain Haun ordered everybody overboard.

But he himself remained. He bade each man farewell, then turned and re-entered the conning-tower, still smoking a cigar, still aboard the ship which had been placed in his command and which he refused to leave while it remained above water.

Both *Glasgow* and *Cornwall* had lowered two boats, and while the search for survivors went on, *Leipzig* lay further and further over to port until the sea flooded in through the casemates and at last quenched the fires and cooled the white-hot metal within her. Her bows dipped, the starboard propeller lifted high out of the water, and at 9.23 p.m. she vanished from sight, wreathed in smoke and steam, and leaving a spreading stain on the sea and a yellow fog above it.

Five officers and thirteen non-commissioned officers and men were picked up alive, the shock of the immersion having killed the others who jumped overboard at the end.

There was very little exultation on the British ships when the *Leipzig* went down, for she had fought gallantly until the end and no ship could have done better against such odds. In particular, the death of Captain Haun was regretted, for the traditions of the Royal Navy have been formed by such men as he : the world of sailors was the poorer for his loss.

CHAPTER ELEVEN

IMMEDIATELY the main action between the heavy ships of the two squadrons had finished, and while *Gneisenau*'s survivors were still being brought aboard, *Invincible*'s signallers began calling up the other ships of Admiral Sturdee's command so as to enable him to assess the strategic position which now obtained in the area. Unfortunately, *Kent*'s transmitting gear had been wrecked shortly before six o'clock by a shell exploding in her wireless room, and the Admiral was not to learn of the destruction of *Nürnberg* until the following afternoon; but *Glasgow*'s signals made it quite apparent that *Leipzig*'s hours were numbered—and also that *Dresden* had escaped.

Sturdee wasted no time.

There seemed to be two courses open to *Dresden* in the immediate future, of which the more likely one for her to follow was to make for the Horn and endeavour to hide herself in some of the innumerable bays and channels around Tierra del Fuego. As soon as *Gneisenau*'s survivors had been picked up, therefore, Sturdee ordered the two battle-cruisers to make for the area at full speed in order to cut her off (and *Nürnberg* too if she had managed to elude *Kent*), and in case either of the German ships had swung north and east instead of south and west, he ordered *Carnarvon* away to meet and to stand guard over his fleet colliers, still coming south to the Falklands under the protection of *Orama*.

As far as the German auxiliaries were concerned, two of them had already been caught, and the third one had disappeared so completely as to raise doubts as to the accuracy of the report that there had been three of them off Port Pleasant.

What in fact had happened was that immediately the imminence of a battle had become obvious, *Seydlitz*—whose duties included that of hospital ship for the German squadron—obeyed her general instructions for action, left the two colliers *Baden* and *Santa Isabel*, and steamed hard after the warships in order to take her position on the disengaged side of the squadron. At noon she was some fifteen miles astern of the cruisers, and altering course south-wards, in obedience to a signal from von Spee ordering all auxiliaries to a new rendezvous. Such was her speed and good fortune that no one on either *Bristol* or *Macedonia* ever set eyes on her.

She continued southward during the day, the thunder and flash of battle away on her port beam. By 8 p.m. she found herself some four miles west of the action between *Cornwall* and *Leipzig*, but was not seen by anyone on the British ships and so quickly made off to the eastward into the thickening mist. Just before midnight she heard signals from the *Dresden* calling up the auxiliaries, but though she acknowledged them, no instructions were received from the light cruiser and in any case the proximity and persistence of the British wireless messages made it obvious that silence on the part of the remaining German vessels was the wisest course.

Eventually her captain decided to take her north to the Argentine coast, where some weeks later she was interned.

But the colliers had not been so fortunate. They saw *Bristol* turn towards them and *Macedonia* come out and join her, and with the reigning conditions of weather and visibility, their only hope lay in possible protection from their own warships. They made as good speed as was possible after the cruisers, but by 3 p.m. *Bristol* had closed up and fired a round across *Baden*'s bows. There was nothing to do but to accept the inevitable.

By 5 p.m. the crews of both colliers were aboard the British ships, and despite the fact that *Baden* and *Santa Isabel* were obviously not transports as Admiral Sturdee had surmised, Captain Fanshawe decided to obey his orders to the letter and both ships were sunk by gunfire. As, between them, they carried several thousand tons of coal and a considerable cargo of provisions, they would in fact have made a valuable and welcome capture.

By 9.30 p.m. when Admiral Sturdee learned of the final end of *Leipzig*, his two battle-cruisers were heading south at eighteen knots, *Bristol* had been ordered to join them, and the task which still lay ahead appeared to be the finding of two enemy light cruisers and possibly one auxiliary. With *Glasgow* and *Cornwall* now disengaged, the Admiral could take further steps to close the avenues of escape to the south, and he ordered Captain Luce to take both ships to Cape Virgins and search or close the eastern entrance to the Magellan Straits.

Taking into consideration the amount of coal which the German light cruisers must have burned during the action, and the fact that their colliers were sunk, it thus seemed probable that the fate of the whole German squadron was sealed—and indeed it must have appeared very much like that to Captain Ludecke of the *Dresden*, as his ship ran on southwards into the night. But the day of catastrophe for the East Asiatic Squadron was at an end, and luck changed for those still at liberty.

Early on the morning of 9 December, it became obvious to Captain Luce that both *Glasgow* and *Cornwall* must return immediately to Port Stanley, the first to refill her magazines and the second her bunkers—for *Cornwall*, like *Kent*, had not coaled since her journey down. Thus Magellan at least was left open for *Dresden*. Then in the early evening of the day following the battle, *Invincible* and *Inflexible* ran into thick fog as they were approaching the Horn. It was this fog which in fact saved *Dresden* for the moment, for she also was making for the Horn—and having no other refuge, she carried on and eventually found temporary haven in Scholl Bay at the head of the Cockburn Channel.

But Sturdee was not so desperate and his battle-cruisers, from his country's point of view, were more valuable than *Dresden*—so he turned back towards the Falklands, searched the waters and bays along their southern coastline, and reached Port Stanley on the morning of 10 December. Here he found *Kent*, and at last heard the story of the end of the *Nürnberg*.

It was time to take stock.

The processes of emotion are much quicker than those of thought. The first reaction through Sturdee's fleet to the realization of victory was 'Thank God we have avenged Kit Cradock!' It was some time later that the strategic effects of the battle came under consideration, and then, not unnaturally, it was discussed mostly from the point of view of their own immediate situation.

One conclusion was fairly generally drawn, and that was that the battle-cruisers would soon be recalled to Home Waters—for by the events of one day it seemed that enemy naval strength outside the Baltic and the Mediterranean had been virtually destroyed. What, despite the lesson of Coronel, appeared miraculous, was the almost trifling cost of the victory.

Four of the enemy's warships had been sunk, over two thousand of their most competent and, it was agreed, courageous seamen had been killed—whilst the British had lost no ships and their total casualties were ten killed or died of wounds, and fifteen wounded. Damage to the ships was inconsiderable, *Kent* receiving the most hits (thirty-seven), and the most damage, as she went in to a much closer range than the others in order to finish off her opponent. *Inflexible* had only been hit three times though she had one man killed and three wounded, whereas *Invincible*, hit twenty-three times, had no casualties at all. *Cornwall* had been hit eighteen times—once under water, which caused the flooding of a bunker; and *Glasgow* six times, none of which caused serious damage. Except for the episode on *Kent* already described, there had been practically no danger of fire throughout the entire action. The days at Port Stanley, therefore, despite the coldness of the weather and the rapidity with which Admiral Sturdee insisted that all repairs should be carried out, passed in an atmosphere of great relief and elation.

Then on 13 December came a report that *Dresden* had been at Punta Arenas two days previously, and by the following morning,

Inflexible, Bristol and *Glasgow* were hurrying off to take up the last pursuit.

It was to be a long one, and already plans were afoot at home which were to bear directly upon the ships of Admiral Sturdee's command.

As may well be imagined, the hours which elapsed between the signals announcing respectively the beginning and end of the Battle of the Falkland Islands passed in an atmosphere of some anxiety at Whitehall—especially as the first one, sent by the Governor of the Islands, read as follows :

Admiral Spee arrived at daylight this morning with all his ships and is now in action with Admiral Sturdee's whole fleet, *which was coaling* [author's italics].

The picture conjured up in the minds of all who read it can well be imagined—the point being, of course, that that picture was fairly accurate, so far as the situation inside the harbour was concerned. However, only two hours elapsed between that telegram and the one announcing the virtual destruction of the East Asiatic Squadron, so that the torment of uncertainty in the minds of Mr Churchill and his associates at the Admiralty, though sharp, was mercifully short. The relief occasioned by the arrival of the second signal was of course, immense—not only from the point of view of the men and ships actually engaged, but also on the much wider field of the naval war.

Within twenty-four hours [Mr Churchill was to write later] orders were sent to a score of British ships to return to Home Waters. For the first time we saw ourselves possessed of immense surpluses of ships of certain classes, of trained men and of naval supplies of all kinds, and were in a position to use them to the best advantage.

Immediately the news was released to the world, Britain's prestige—indissolubly linked for centuries with that of her Navy—rose again. Friendly neutrals addressed glowing messages of congratulations to her consulates, and ones which had been unfriendly let it be known that those matters upon which there had seemed to be some disagreement during the past few months, were again open for discussion as it appeared that there had been misunderstandings of a trifling nature.

Most important of all, mercantile shipping moved with greater confidence across the oceans, and a large proportion of it was carrying food and war materials toward Allied ports. There was still some danger to be faced of course, for the fate of the *Karlsruhe* had not become known (she had blown up with an internal explosion on 4 November) and the *Dresden* was still at large, but at least her general position was known, and it could surely not be long before she was hunted down and caught.

And with this in mind, that incredible old man Lord Fisher spent much time examining all information in connection with the battle as it came in, deciding to his own satisfaction that Sturdee's tactics during the battle had been wrong, and on 11 December he announced that Sturdee should be kept down in the South Atlantic until he had finished the job and caught *Dresden*. As the battle-cruisers were needed at home, Sturdee should transfer his flag to the old *Carnarvon*!

When Mr Churchill disagreed and firmly vetoed the suggestion, the First Sea Lord was 'for some time much vexed at my decision'.

It is interesting however, to read the criticisms which Lord Fisher at the time—and many others since—had to make of Admiral Sturdee's conduct of the battle.

Fisher's main attack rested on the escape of *Dresden*—rather from the Nelsonic point of view : 'Now, had we taken ten sail, and had allowed the eleventh to escape when it had been possible to have got at her, I could never have called it well done.' An admirable sentiment for the man on the spot who thus sets himself the highest standards, but an objective viewpoint should see—and acknowledge—that eighty per cent success in battle is an achievement of merit. In any case, the escape of *Dresden* was the result of a choice made by Captain Luce of *Glasgow*, and although the official responsibility was undoubtedly Sturdee's, few reasonable people would affirm that the blame was too.

In any case, was it a matter for blame?

When Captain Luce first engaged *Leipzig*, it appeared to him that neither *Cornwall* nor *Kent* was developing sufficient speed to catch either her or *Nürnberg*—and by the time that the County cruisers were in a position to fire effectively on *Leipzig* (as a result of *Glasgow*'s delaying tactics, it should be remembered) the *Dresden* was so far away as to render it impossible for *Glasgow* to catch her before nightfall. There is a possibility—not very great, but real nonetheless—that had *Glasgow* continued after *Dresden*, both she *and Leipzig* might have kept their distance from their pursuers until late evening, when mists and darkness would have aided them.

Of the other criticisms made of Admiral Sturdee's tactics during the battle, it would seem that the most valid is the one that he did not use his advantages in speed to secure the lee position, and that he seemed to be little aware of the difficulty caused to the gun-layers aboard *Invincible*, and especially *Inflexible*, by the flagship's smoke. Certainly Captain Phillimore's action in taking *Inflexible* out of the smoke and across towards the *Gneisenau*—without orders—is a reflection upon this aspect of his admiral's handling of the two battle-cruisers. It is pleasant to record that, after the action, Admiral Sturdee gave his full approval to the move.

The criticism that whereas von Spee took only an hour to defeat Cradock, Sturdee took practically all day to defeat von Spee, is upon examination more valid as a criticism of British naval construction than of Sturdee's tactics. To a certain extent, it can be said that both admirals gained their victories in the time available for doing so, and von Spee was aided in this by the fact that, rightly or wrongly, Cradock made no attempt to run. If von Spee had followed Cradock's example, it may well be that the Falklands battle would have been over much quicker—and for himself, possibly more satisfactorily.

That Sturdee was justified in ensuring that none of *Scharnhorst*'s excellently-grouped salvoes should land on *Invincible*'s decks, was proved only too tragically eighteen months later at Jutland, when just such an event happened, and the battle-cruiser blew up with the loss of Admiral Hood and practically all the officers and men. It was certainly a salvo of heavier calibre shells than *Scharnhorst* could have fired which initiated this disaster, but the real cause was in the design of the British ship, which would allow flash from shell bursting in quite a number of exposed places to travel through hoists and along passages and into the magazines.

Defence, *Warrior* and *Black Prince* were all to meet fates as instant and overwhelming as that of *Invincible*, yet the German ships—at Falklands and in the North Sea—took incredible punishment, and the majority were only sent to the bottom by internal demolitions carried out by their own crews. Britain's reputation for ship-building seems to rest on her mercantile, as distinct from naval, construction, and it is interesting to recall that even in the days of the Napoleonic Wars, a British captain who was given command of a captured French warship considered himself very fortunate. In some fields Britain's naval designers seem very slow to learn.

The superiority of German telescopes and range-finders in 1914 was another factor which could have received more attention than apparently it did—and there was another weakness which Raeder misinterpreted when he wrote the official German account of the cruiser actions in *Cruiser Warfare*, between the wars. When comparing the British and German accounts of the actions and also the charts showing the various movements of the ships concerned, he announces rather smugly that German officers systematically plotted the speeds and courses of all ships at all times thus ensuring accuracy, whereas the British seemed to have neglected this duty. 'It may be surmised from these facts,' he claims, 'that in spite of the overwhelming superiority of their armament [at Falklands], great anxiety and uneasiness prevailed among them.'

What in fact did take place was that on *Inflexible* at least, an officer carefully noted the ship's speed and course every minute—but when the readings were later plotted on to the charts it was found that gunfire had affected the ship's magnetism, which in turn affected the compass-readings. These were later found sometimes to have been as much as ninety degrees out, for although the German armoured cruisers were fitted with gyroscopic compasses at that time, the British battle-cruisers were still using magnetic compasses.

The British did, however, have a decided superiority in the ammunition used at the Falklands, for the explosion of the lyddite shells aboard the German ships undoubtedly caused immeasurably more devastation than the 'common' shell, or the German high explosive on Cradock's squadron at Coronel. But time was to prove that even here there was no great cause for satisfaction, for at Jutland, against the German battleships, these shells broke up without piercing the heavy armour.

German writers on the cruiser war have other criticisms to make of British tactics and behaviour. In particular they bitterly attack the British commanders for the fact that no survivors from *Scharnhorst* were picked up, and very few from *Nürnberg* or *Leipzig*. As they also claim, in virtually the same breath, that no German ship surrendered, their arguments seem to be attempts to have the best both ways. They cite the scenes of horror and bloodshed which undoubtedly took place aboard Captain Haun's ship at the end—without apparently pausing to reflect that had there been any survivors from *Monmouth*, they may well have had similar stories to tell.

There is some truth in the assertion that in the early months of the Great War, the German naval commanders acted upon several occasions with commendable chivalry—but this may not be unconnected with the fact that they did so aboard ships sufficiently well-built to allow them to take risks. No last desperate shot from *Good Hope* or *Monmouth* could have blown *Scharnhorst* or *Gneisenau* to pieces, whereas it is possible that only the presence of mind of Sergeant Mayes saved *Kent* in the last minutes of her fight with *Nürnberg*.

In any case, even in those days, war was to the death or to surrender, and a ship remained in action until either she was sunk or until she hauled down her flag. And it seems that this latter course was followed by none of von Spee's warships on 8 December, 1914 —all credit to him and to the men under his command.

With regard to von Spee's tactics, much has been made by naval writers of his failure to attack Admiral Sturdee's fleet while it was still penned in harbour at Port Stanley. Had the first lieutenant of *Gneisenau* been believed when he first reported the presence of tripod masts in the harbour, then possibly this is the course which von Spee would have followed—it certainly constituted the only hope his squadron had of inflicting severe damage on the British ships. But from German accounts it seems that until those tripod masts were seen by officers aboard the *Leipzig* at ten o'clock, Admiral von Spee was not informed of the presence of the battle-cruisers. By then, *Gneisenau* and *Nürnberg* were already withdrawing, *Scharnhorst* was leading the other light cruisers away, and the British ships were coming out after them.

As for the contention that he should have arrived in force off the entrance to Port Stanley at dawn, it is as well to remember that darkness on the night of 7/8 December lasted only some three hours. With the conditions of light and weather which obtained during the crucial hours, it is probable that had he attempted this, his ships, or at least their smoke, would have been seen at dusk by someone on the island—if not a naval look-out, then perhaps one of the crofters. One officer on Admiral Stoddart's staff has stated that they were in fact seen, but as the German ships must then have been a hundred miles away from Port Stanley, it could only have been the result of either imagination or a mirage.

The loss of the German ships off the Falkland Islands seems thus to have been brought about by basically the same factor which caused the loss of the British ships off Coronel—lack of information as to the enemy's position and strength. In von Spee's case, he also lacked accurate information with regard to stores of fuel and provisions which his own countrymen were arranging for his use, and the combination of the telegram from Buenos Aires stating that coal would not be available on the east coast of South America, and the repeated rumour that Port Stanley with all its coal stores was virtually unguarded, left him with little choice but to go there.

Weaknesses in the German supply and intelligence organizations, and the obstinacy of Lord Fisher in insisting that the battle-cruisers left Devonport when they did, thus served to decide the day—and it is not inapt in this regard, to quote a passage which appeared in a German newspaper after Coronel.

> The superiority of our fleet in no way detracts from the glory of our victory, for the very essence of the business of a strategist is the marshalling of a superior fleet at the right place, at the right moment.

During the days immediately following the Battle of the Falkland Islands, Admiral Sturdee received a succession of telegrams from Whitehall, each one countermanding the orders contained in the last, in view of contradicting rumours and reports of the *Dresden*'s movements. Eventually the need for the battle-cruisers in more northern waters became paramount, and on 16 December *Invincible*, still—despite Lord Fisher's opinion—flying Admiral Sturdee's flag, left Port Stanley. *Inflexible* had by this time reached the Pacific, while *Glasgow* and *Bristol* were still ferreting through the bays and channels of the western end of Magellan Straits, and when on 19 December it seemed that *Dresden* had, for the moment, succeeded in giving her pursuers the slip, *Inflexible* too, turned back for home.

Admiral Stoddart was left in command of British naval forces operating from Port Stanley, and during the last days of 1914 and the first weeks of 1915, his ship steamed up innumerable fjords and searched numberless bays and channels for the elusive *Dresden*. They found ample evidence of her continued existence, but none, fortunately, of any aggressive spirit, for Captain Ludecke appeared to have no ambition to rival the deeds of his brother captains aboard *Emden* or *Karlsruhe*; in the seven and a half months of her wartime career, she captured only four British merchantmen—and one of those was carrying a German cargo.

But she did contrive to keep herself out of sight of her pursuers for a surprisingly long period. It was three months to the day after she had vanished into the evening mists off the Falklands, leaving *Leipzig* and *Nürnberg* to their fate, that she was suddenly sighted from the decks of *Kent*. She had, during that time, been chased away from the indented coastline, and the place where *Kent* found her was up almost abreast of Coronel and due south of Más-a-Fuera—but unfortunately, *Dresden*'s boilers were in far better condition than *Nürnberg*'s had been, and this time it was the German ship who was light and riding high out of the water.

Kent was unable to close with her and *Dresden* disappeared into the evening with the same celerity which she had shown off the Falklands.

But there are not many places in that part of the world where a warship obviously short of fuel can hide—especially when searching vessels have arranged a careful watch on all ships which might conceivably be acting as colliers for her. On the morning of 14 March, acting as a result of intercepted wireless messages and a process of deduction and elimination, Captain Luce in *Glasgow* led *Kent* and *Orama* around the point of Cumberland Bay on the coast of Juan Fernandez Island. *Dresden* lay anchored five hundred yards from the shore, flying her ensign and jack, smoke issuing from her funnels, and as the British ships approached, *Dresden*'s guns were cleared away and trained upon them.

What happened then was so out of character with the behaviour of the other German warships which have figured in this narrative, that it comes as something of a relief to remember that *Dresden* had not been an original member of the East Asiatic Squadron, and her complement had only served under Admiral von Spee for eight weeks and one day.

'An action ensued,' reads the announcement later made by the Secretary of the Admiralty. 'After five minutes' fighting the *Dresden* hauled down her colours and displayed the white flag.'

There followed details of the explosion of her magazine, the care and treatment of her fifteen casualties (all wounded) and the statement that there were no British casualties and no damage to British ships.

Excellent reasons can doubtless be advanced for Captain

Ludecke's conduct of *Dresden*'s war—but not in a book which deals with the exploits of such men as Luce and von Schönberg, Haun, Brandt of *Monmouth* and Allen of *Kent*, Maerker, Verner, and Admirals Graf von Spee and Sir Christopher Cradock. In that context, such explanations sound hollow and rather specious.

By this time it had become evident that whatever the fate of *Karlsruhe*, she was no longer a factor to be reckoned with, and within a month the last of the enemy armed merchant cruisers was chased into neutral waters and duly interned.

Britannia, at the end of April 1915, undoubtedly ruled the waves —and except for those few people who seriously contemplated the possibility of a European power waging unrestricted submarine warfare, it appeared to the world that she would continue to do so. There were rumours of a slight check to some Royal Naval intentions in the Eastern Mediterranean on 18 March, but already in the Great War, Britain had demonstrated that she would win in the end.

But other weapons and other methods of warfare were being developed by other countries, and if the battles of Coronel and the Falklands were the first major fleet actions fought by the Royal Navy since the days of sail, they were also the last which any navy would fight in two dimensions. From now on, mines, submarines and aerial bombardments were hazards which brought new factors into sea warfare and caused, eventually, a new approach to naval tactics. They also brought about conditions which, somewhat tardily, caused a collaboration between British scientist, engineer and naval constructor—and more important still, a systematic study of naval strategy which had been conspicuously lacking before.

Coronel was not repeated at the beginning of the second World War.

There was instead the Battle of the River Plate.

APPENDIX

THE following communications passed between Naval Staff Head-
quarters in Berlin, Admiral Graf von Spee, the ships under his
command, or the various German agencies in Africa or the
Americas, between 1 November 1914 and the sinking of the
Scharnhorst on 8 December :

1 November : *Graf von Spee to Naval Staff.*
Have concentrated our five cruisers. *Prinz Eitel Friedrich* has ordered
coal at Valparaiso for 4 November.

2 November : *Graf von Spee to all ships.*
By the Grace of God a fine victory. My thanks and good wishes to
the crews.

Graf von Spee to Titania.
Tow the captured sailing-vessel *Helicon* to Más-a-Fuera and close
Dresden en route. *Dresden* will take over your duties as regards
San Sacramento.

Graf von Spee to Dresden.
On signal 'Detach' you are to get in touch with *Titania.* She has
received orders today in 30°12′S 76°31′W to take the commandeered
Norwegian sailing-vessel to Más-a-Fuera. The first wireless telegraph
call is to be made after daybreak on 3 November. In addition you will
take over the duty of seizing the *Sacramento*, reference Operation
Order of 29 October, and bringing her to Más-a-Fuera instead of the
rendezvous there given. Use Marconi for wireless telegraph signals.

Graf von Spee to Leipzig.

On the signal 'Detach' you are to search for the colliers 150 miles west (True) from Valparaiso and escort them to Más-a-Fuera. You and *Dresden* will coal there. *Scharnhorst, Gneisenau* and *Nürnberg* will call at Valparaiso on 3 November and will sail from there to coal at Más-a-Fuera.

3 November : *Received from Naval Staff by Graf von Spee.*

Lines of rendezvous in the Atlantic are all compromised, all trade routes being strongly patrolled. In the Atlantic cruiser warfare can only be carried on by ships operating in groups. *Karlsruhe* and *Kronprinz Wilhelm* have orders to combine. It is intended to concentrate all forces and order them to break through for home in groups.

Naval Staff to Graf von Spee (probably received at Más-a-Fuera).

For cruiser squadron. You are advised to try to break through with all your ships for home.

Graf von Spee to Naval Staff.

On 1 November I defeated the British ships *Good Hope, Monmouth, Glasgow* and auxiliary *Otranto* off Coronel, with *Scharnhorst, Gneisenau, Leipzig* and *Dresden*. *Nürnberg* was detached during the action. Heavy sea. I opened fire at 11,400 yards and silenced their guns. Action lasted eighty-four minutes. I ceased fire at nightfall. *Good Hope* severely damaged by gunfire and explosion. Disappeared in the darkness. *Monmouth* chased and found by *Nürnberg*. She had a heavy list. *Nürnberg* opened fire and she capsized. Rescue work impossible owing to heavy sea and lack of boats. *Glasgow* escaped apparently slightly damaged. The auxiliary cruiser got out of range after the first hit and escaped. No losses on our side, damage inconsiderable.

4 November : *Commander von Knorr to Valparaiso* (arrived 5 November).

I have requested the Naval Staff to despatch a Seydlitz class cruiser to the North Atlantic to support the cruiser squadron. This is probably being proceeded with. Strictest secrecy necessary.

[*Note* : Von Spee probably received news of this at Más-a-Fuera.]

9 November : *Buenos Aires to Valparaiso.*

Inform cruiser squadron that coal cannot be sent in steamers from Argentine and Brazilian ports, coal export being prohibited. East coast of South America is importing coal from North America only. If the cruiser squadron comes to the east coast it would be advisable for it to bring as many colliers as possible in company.

[*Note* : It is uncertain how much information regarding coal did reach von Spee. According to Raeder, he did receive a telegram from Naval Staff (untraceable) stating that supplies from Europe were being arranged, and it is believed that he was informed of the contents of the above signal just before he left Penas Gulf.]

11 November : *Received in Valparaiso from Commander von Knorr.*
If the cruiser squadron decides to return home, it appears advisable for her to leave immediately. In my opinion it is dangerously situated.

12 November : *Received in Valparaiso from New York.*
A letter from Naval Staff dated 10 October has in essentials the same contents as their letter of 29 September providing for a break-through for home. . . . It gives further details regarding coaling arrangements in the Atlantic, the general dislocation of the enemy, and about German wireless telegraph stations and call signs.

13 November : *San Francisco to Valparaiso.*
Have received an important communication from the Naval Staff regarding British commerce protection in the Atlantic and containing information of value for a break-through to the North Sea. Will repeat telegram in full as soon as possible.

[*Note* : *Leipzig* and *Dresden* were at Valparaiso when this telegram arrived and presumably passed the information to von Spee upon arrival at Penas Gulf. Attempts to send the whole contents of the letter to him failed however, and it was then sent to La Plata, who sent it on down to Santa Elena for collection by von Spee upon arrival. He thus never received it.]

Graf von Spee to Naval Staff (received 16 November).
Leipzig reports that one hour before *Monmouth* capsized, some of the crew observed that *Leipzig* was passing through wreckage, hammocks and floating corpses in the position where *Good Hope* had last been sighted. This goes to prove that *Good Hope* was sunk.

About 14 November :
Valparaiso received telegram from West Africa supply base to the effect that a steamer with 4,000 tons of coal was waiting at Palma and four steamers with 8,000 tons at Teneriffe.

15 November : *Punta Arenas to Valparaiso.*
British steamer from the Falkland Islands reports no warships there. They have been ordered to South Africa where a revolution has broken out. The mail steamer remained at Port Stanley for half an hour and did not unload as she feared a German attack.
[*Note* : Valparaiso annotated this telegram : 'Believe this to be English bluff and have not repeated it as it would not influence cruiser squadron's dispositions.' But the same report also reached Berlin on 18 November via Buenos Aires, and *Dresden* officers subsequently stated that von Spee received report at San Quentin Bay.]

16 November : *Received by Graf von Spee from Naval Staff.*
What are your plans? How much ammunition have you?

Graf von Spee to Naval Staff (received 19 November).
The cruiser squadron intends to break through for home.

17 November : *Graf von Spee to Naval Staff* (received 21 November).
Supply of ammunition is as follows. Each large cruiser has 445 rounds heavy ammunition and 1,100 rounds secondary ammunition. Light cruisers 1,860 rounds.

18 November : *Received Valparaiso via San Francisco from Naval Staff.*
Impossible to dispatch a large cruiser from home to the North Atlantic.
[*Note* : Raeder considers it unlikely that von Spee was ever informed of this message.]

Graf von Spee via Valparaiso to La Plata and New York.
Send steamers, German if possible, to arrive at Port Santa Elena on 5 December with 10,000 tons of coal and provisions for a thousand men for three months. No oil. Intelligence reports particularly desirable.

Graf von Spee to Naval Staff.
New York and La Plata are to arrange together for the dispatch of 20,000 tons of coal, 5,000 to await orders at Pernambuco from 1 January, 15,000 at New York from 20 January. From New York also provisions for two thousand men for three months, but only half the oil given in general instructions.

20 November : La Plata received a report from Rio de Janeiro that the guns of *Canopus* had been mounted on the Falkland Islands.

21 November : *Naval Staff to Valparaiso* (received 23 November). According to the press a British squadron consisting of ten ships has been sighted three hundred miles from Montevideo. Take all possible steps to warn cruiser squadron. Inform Punta Arenas.
[*Note* : Raeder considers that the message was probably not received by von Spee.]

24 November :
Graf von Spee verbally instructed Lieutenant zur Helle [of *Amasis*] to endeavour to check truth of message to the effect that Falkland Islands had been abandoned by the British.

Rio de Janeiro reported to La Plata that *Invincible*, *Defence* and *Carnarvon* were off Abrolhos Rocks.
[*Note* : La Plata apparently made no attempt to telegraph this information to von Spee, but included it in dispatches to await him at Santa Elena.]

Valparaiso to Naval Staff to the effect that von Spee intended to reach Egg Harbour on 5 December, and had summoned steamers from Santa Elena to arrive afterwards so as not to indicate his own destination beforehand. Last line reads : 'Coal and provisions from Chile are therefore no longer under consideration.'

La Plata to Valparaiso.
As the colliers expected have not arrived, we shall probably be unable to send 10,000 tons of coal to Port Santa Elena. Can you inform cruiser squadron?

25 November : *Valparaiso to La Plata.*
Will try to inform squadron re colliers for Santa Elena. If their dispatch proves impossible, please endeavour at least to send provisions and news as arranged, and also a complete list of colliers and storeships available on the east coast.

30 November :
La Plata reported to Valparaiso that the following steamers could be sent to Santa Elena : *Elinore Woermann* with provisions and equipment

and about 1,700 tons of coal, to leave Buenos Aires on 2 December. *Patagonia* with provisions and equipment and 1,200–1,500 tons, to leave Montevideo on 2 December. *Mera* with 1,200–1,600 tons to leave Montevideo on 3 December. *Gottia* with provisions and about 1,400 tons to follow on 7 or 8 December. Neutral *Josephina* expected with 1,500 tons of coal on 9 December. *Sierra Cordoba* would be ready for sea about the middle of December. Also detailed intelligence reports and Naval Staff letter of 10 October would be waiting at Santa Elena.

1 December : *Naval Staff to Graf von Spee* (awaiting him at Santa Elena).
Where shall the ammunition vessels be sent to? They will be ready for sea in the second half of December.

2 December :
Von Spee to *Dresden* to the effect that she would be given a chance to replace coal lost *en route*, possibly at the Falkland Islands.

6/7 December :
Lieutenant zur Helle (*Amasis*) signalled Flag to the effect that the rumour regarding abandonment of Falkland Islands considered 'very probable'.

7/8 December :
Von Spee sent lengthy signal to *Elinore Woermann* (text unavailable).

8 December : Signals throughout action.

0930. *Flag to* Gneisenau.
Do not accept action. Concentrate on course east by north. Proceed at full speed.

0940. *Flag to all ships.*
Get up steam in all boilers.

1200. *Flag to auxiliaries.*
Rendezvous at 54°S 57°W.

1320. *Flag to light cruisers.*
Part company. Endeavour to escape.

Flag to Gneisenau.
Follow your leader.

1500.   *Flag to* Seydlitz.
Former anchorage.

Approx. 1515.   Gneisenau *to Flag*.
Why is the Admiral's flag at half-mast? Is the Admiral dead?

Graf von Spee to Captain Maerker.
No. I am all right so far. Have you hit anything?

Captain Maerker to Graf von Spee.
The smoke prevents all observation.

Graf von Spee to Captain Maerker.
You were right after all.

1555.   *Flag to* Gneisenau.
Endeavour to escape if your engines are still intact.

Aboukir, H.M.S., 38, 114

Abrolhos Rocks, 33, 48

Admiralty, the: and responsibility for Coronel, 23, 24, 31–7; directions to Cradock, 32–3

See also Churchill, Winston; Fisher, Lord

Ahlers, 80

Allen, Captain (H.M.S. *Kent*), 112, 138, 142–4, 153, 168

Amasis, collier, 64, 68, 72, 80, 90, 97

Aneker, Lieutenant, 132, 136

Asama, 43

Australia, H.M.S., 43, 45, 60

Baden, collier, 64, 68, 72, 80, 96, 108, 157

Bankfields, S.S., 59

Beresford, Lord Charles, 40, 47

Berndt, Sub-Lieutenant, 145–6

Berwick, H.M.S., 45

Black Prince, H.M.S., 163

Botticher, Commander von, 74

Brandt, Captain (H.M.S. *Monmouth*), 168

Bremen, 95

Breslau, 39

Bristol, H.M.S., 48, 50, 91, 157; at Port Stanley, 102, 109; pursues *Dresden*, 160, 166

Bülow, Lieut-Commander von, 145–6

Canopus, H.M.S., 4–5, 7–8, 23, 27–8, 32–3, 35, 40, 42, 45, 65–6, 70, 91–2; attempts to join forces with *Glasgow*, 19–21; at Port Stanley, 22; range of her guns, 28; guardship at Port Stanley, 45, 94; engages *Gneisenau*, 101, 103, 105–6

Carnarvon, H.M.S., 34, 43, 45, 48, 50, 82, 91; at Port Stanley, 102; FALKLAND ISLANDS: 108, 119, 133; ordered for action, 107; tries to come up with flagship, 110–11; opens fire, 130; rescues survivors from *Gneisenau*, 135; guards colliers, 156

Chonos Archipelago, 19

Churchill, Winston, 38; and the battle of Coronel, 24, 27, 35–7, 39; and Fisher, 41–2; orders battle cruisers to foreign service, 43–4; directive to C.-in-C., Devonport, 46; on Admiral Sturdee, 46; and the battle of the Falkland Isles, 160; vetoes transfer of Sturdee's flag, 161

Condé, 45

Corbett, Sir Julian, *Official History of Naval Operations of the Great War*, 24

Corcovado Bay, 76

Cornwall, H.M.S., 43, 45, 48, 50, 82, 91; at Port Stanley, 102, 105; FALKLAND ISLANDS: 107, 108, 110, 147, 162; pursues escaping light cruisers, 112, 137–9; draws nearer *Leipzig*, 148–9; engages *Leipzig*, 149–150, 157; reopens fire, 153; rescues survivors from *Leipzig*, 155; returns to Port Stanley, 158; damage to, 159

Coronel, Battle of: *Glasgow* leaves Coronel Bay, 1–3; comparative forces, 3–4; British hope of meeting isolated enemy units, 4; British squadron forms line abreast, 5–6; German force sighted, 6; Cradock orders turn away to the south, 7; von Spee avoids action, 7; inequality of opposing forces, 8; Cradock decides to attack, 8–9; German ships open fire, 9, 11; *Good Hope* and *Monmouth* hit, 11; *Otranto* departs unscathed, 11; *Monmouth* pounded by *Gneisenau*, 12–13; *Good Hope* badly damaged, and explodes, 13–15; *Glasgow* little damaged, 15–16; *Glasgow* engages four enemy ships, 16; *Monmouth* halted, 16; *Glasgow* races for Magellan Straits, 16; *Nürnberg* sinks *Monmouth*, 17–18; British reaction to the defeat, 23; alleged Admiralty responsibility, 23–4, 31–7; Cradock's decision to accept action, 27–30; Cradock's tactics, 30–1

Cradock, Rear-Admiral Sir Christopher, 2, 4, 15, 39, 42, 48–9, 60–2, 65–6, 76, 110, 162, 168; CORONEL: aims to destroy *Leipzig*, 5; orders formation of battle-line, 6; orders turn away to the south, 7; re-forms battle line, 7; decides to attack, 8–9; brings *Monmouth* into action, 12; holds converging course, 13; criticized for accepting action, and for tactics, 23, 27–31; Admiralty directives to, 32–3; strategic error, 34;

exchanges with the Admiralty, 34–7.
—Education and career, 24–7; his
book *Whispers from the Fleet*, 25, 26
Cressy, H.M.S., 39, 114
Cumberland, H.M.S., 82

Dartmouth, H.M.S., 43
Defence, H.M.S., 34, 45, 48, 92, 163;
armament, 33; ordered to Cradock's
support, 42–3
De Wet, Christian, 50
Dresden, 27, 32, 33, 54, 57, 59–60
62–4, 68, 71, 74, 76, 80; CORONEL:
4, 7–8, 11, 16.—In the Horn passage,
88, 93; at Picton Island, 96; moves
to attack Port Stanley, 99; flight
from Port Stanley, 101; FALKLAND
ISLANDS: escapes, 137–8, 148, 156,
158, 161–2, 166–7; calls up auxiliaries, 157; interned, 157; surrenders
and scuttles, 167–8
Drummuir, S.S., 94, 96

East Asiatic Squadron, German, 2–4
9, 32, 50–1, 61, 64, 79; at Coronel
(*see* Coronel, Battle of); at Más-a-
Fuera, 68–72; in San Quentin
Sound, 76; coaling problems, 79–
81; rounds the Horn, 85–94; at
Picton Island, 94–7; moves to attack
Port Stanley, 97–101 (*see* Falkland
Isles, Battle of the)
Easter Island, 60
Ebeling, Captain, 76, 90
Elinore Woermann, auxiliary vessel, 98
Elsinore, S.S., 59
Emden, 31, 57, 59, 69, 80, 166
Encounter, H.M.S., 45
Erckerdt, German minister at Val-
paraiso, 64
Excellent, H.M.S. (Royal Naval Gun-
nery Establishment), 28

Falkland Islands: coaling station for
British warships, 22; reported as
unguarded, 78
See also Port Stanley
Falkland Islands, Battle of the:
German squadron approaches Port
Stanley, 97–100; British ships
sighted, and Germans turn away,
100–1; the British warships in Port
Stanley, 102–5; 'Action' sounded,
105–6; first shots, 106; British move
out of harbour, 106–8; German
position and movements reported,

108–10; general order to engage,
110; von Spee orders light cruisers
to escape, 110; main forces engaged,
111; ranges open out, and firing
ceases, 111–12; Germans fly southwards, 112–13; excellence of German gunnery, 113–14; the range
closes, 114–15, 117–18; *Scharnhorst*
on fire, and sinks, 117–18, 123–8;
Gneisenau engages three British
ships, 129–32; end of *Gneisenau*,
132–6; *Nürnberg* attempts to escape,
137–41; her end, 142–6; end of
Leipzig, 146–55; fate of auxiliary
vessels, 156–7; British ships return
to Port Stanley, 158–9; chase of
Dresden, 159–60, 166–7; effect of the
victory on British prestige, 160–1;
Sturdee's tactics criticized, 161–3;
British superiority in ammunition,
164; British behaviour criticized,
164–5; von Spee's tactics criticized,
165; basic cause of German defeat,
165–6; end of *Dresden*, 167–8
Fanshawe, Captain (H.M.S. *Bristol*),
109, 157
Felton, Mrs, 109
Fielitz, Captain, 60, 96
Fisher, Lord, 51, 83; energetic re-
forms by, 40; and Churchill, 40–1;
orders *Defence* to Cradock's support,
41–2; orders battle-cruisers to
foreign service, 43–4, 166; directive
to C.-in-C., Devonport, 46; egotism
and ruthlessness, 47–8; criticizes
Sturdee's tactics at Falkland
Islands, 161

German New Guinea, base at, 32
Gill Bay, 73, 81
Glasgow, H.M.S., 4, 19–21, 33–4, 40,
45, 50, 61, 65, 70, 91; in Coronel
Bay, 1–2; equality with *Leipzig*, 3;
joins the Flag, 5; CORONEL: 7, 9, 11,
54; sights the enemy, 6; comparatively undamaged, 15–16; engages
four enemy ships, 16; cease fire
ordered, and attempts to help *Monmouth*, 16; races for Magellan
Straits, 16, 18.—Joins forces with
Canopus, 21; moves south, 19–21;
at Port Stanley, 22; range of her
guns, 28; at Abrolhos Rocks, 48; at
Port Stanley, 102, 103; FALKLAND
ISLANDS: 109, 156; joins *Kent*, 107;

reports enemy position, 108; pursues escaping light cruisers, 110, 112, 137–9; engages *Leipzig*, 146–54; signals *Leipzig*, 153; rescues survivors, 155; returns to Port Stanley, 158; damage to, 159; pursues *Dresden*, 160, 166–8

Gneisenau, 3, 27, 32–3, 56–7, 62–3, 79, 92; CORONEL: 6–9, 11, 16, 54–5; pounds *Monmouth*, 12–13.—At Más-a-Fuera, 68, 69; rounds the Horn, 85, 86; at Picton Island, 96; moves to attack Port Stanley, 97–101, 103; FALKLAND ISLANDS: 164, 165; turns eastward, 106; ordered to accept action, 110, 122; engaged by *Invincible*, 111; shell-burst on after-deck, 114; engages *Inflexible*, 118, 119, 124, 127, 129; lists, 126; badly damaged, and fights three British ships, 129–32; carnage and devastation on, 133; without fighting power, and scuttled, 133–6

Goeben, 31, 39
Gonzalez Channel, 21
Good Hope, H.M.S. (Cradock's Flagship), 4, 50, 56, 125, 164; in Coronel Bay, 2; joined by *Glasgow*, 5; CORONEL: 6–8, 12, 16, 54–5; foredeck explodes, 11 ; badly damaged, and explodes, 13–15; misunderstanding with the Admiralty, 24. —Range of her guns, 28
Göttingen, 63, 65
Grant, Captain Heathcote (H.M.S. *Canopus*), 19, 20, 21, 22, 45, 105, 106, 109
Gumprecht, German Consul-General at Valparaiso, 64

Haun, Captain (*Leipzig*), 70, 150–5, 168
Hawke, H.M.S., 114
Helicon, S.S., 64, 68–9, 71–2
Helle, Lieutenant zur, 80, 90, 91, 97
Hirst, Lieutenant, 1, 2, 4, 48, 107, 113
Hizen, 36, 45
Hogue, H.M.S., 39, 114
Holmwood, S.S., 59
Hood, Admiral, 163
Hyades, S.S., 59

Idzumo, 36, 43, 45
Inflexible, H.M.S., 46, 48–9, 166; at Abrolhos Rocks, 85; at Port Stanley,

102; FALKLAND ISLANDS: 108–9, 114, 117, 162–3; engages *Leipzig*, 110–11, 118, 121; engages *Gneisenau*, 118–119, 124, 127, 129–31; rescues survivors from *Gneisenau*, 135–6; damage to, 159;. pursues *Dresden*, 160
Invincible, H.M.S., 43, 48, 166; Admiral Sturdee's Flagship, 46; at Abrolhos Rocks, 85, 95; at Port Stanley, 102, 103; FALKLAND ISLANDS : 107–8, 115, 117, 162; engages the enemy, 110, 122; engages *Gneisenau*, 111, 118, 127; hit, 111, 114, 130; engages *Scharnhorst*, 118, 124; damage to, 159

Jerram, Admiral, 32
Johnke, Lieutenant, 148

Kale, Lieut-Commander, 145
Karlsruhe, 31, 32, 161, 166, 168
Kent, H.M.S., 43, 48; at Port Stanley, 100, 102–3; FALKLAND ISLANDS: 106, 110, 147, 156, 162; joined by *Glasgow*, 107; crosses wake of German cruisers, 112; pursues escaping light cruisers, 137–9; engages *Leipzig*, 139; engages *Nürnberg*, 141–4; flash passes down her ammunition-hoist, 143–4; rescues *Nürnberg* survivors, 145–6; draws nearer *Leipzig*, 148–9; engages *Leipzig*, 149; transmitting gear wrecked, 156; returns to Port Stanley, 159; damage to, 159; sights *Dresden*, 167
Knorr, Commander von, 64, 65, 81, 82; 89, 90
Kohler, Warrant Officer, 145
Kotthaus, Lieutenant, 97
Kretschmer, Commander, 149, 152
Lancaster, H.M.S., 45
La Plata, German agency at, 73, 81, 89, 94–5
Leipzig, 1, 4–5, 27, 54, 57, 59, 61–4, 95; equality with *Glasgow*, 3; CORONEL: 7–8, 11, 16; range of her guns, 28; at Más-a-Fuera, 68, 70–1; leaves for Valparaiso, 72; FALKLAND ISLANDS: sights British ships, 101; engaged by *Inflexible*, 110, 121; attempts to escape, 137–9; engaged by *Kent*, 139; engaged by *Glasgow*, 146; hit, 147–8; engaged by *Corn-*

wall and *Kent*, 149–51, 157; fires torpedoes, 151; Captain Haun orders her to be sunk, 152; devastation on, 152–5; sinks, 155
Longmoon, collier, 80
Louis of Battenberg, Admiral Prince, 38–40
Luce, Captain John (H.M.S. *Glasgow*), 1–2, 5, 16, 17, 22, 103, 147, 151–3, 158, 161, 162, 167–8
Ludecke, Captain (*Dresden*), 158, 166–8
Luedtke, Dr, 145
Luxor, collier, 81

Macedonia, H.M.S., 50, 157; at Port Stanley, 100, 102–3; FALKLAND ISLANDS: relieved by *Kent*, 105; attacks transports, 109
Maerker, Captain (*Gneisenau*), 96–8, 100, 105, 106, 120, 122, 125, 129, 134–6, 168
Maltzahn, Baron von, 98
Más-a-Fuera (Juan Fernandez group): von Spee at, 60; sinking of *Titania* at, 63–4; East Asiatic Squadron at, 68–72; coal at, 80
Mayes, Sergeant Charles, 143–4; 164
Memphis, collier, 76, 80
Messier Channel, 20, 21
Meyer, Engineer-Officer, 131, 134, 135
Moltke, 81
Monmouth, H.M.S., 2, 4–6, 33–4, 40, 53, 82, 125, 164; CORONEL: 7–8; foredeck on fire, 11, 54; pounded by *Gneisenau*, 12–13; sunk by *Nürnberg*, 17–18, 55–6
Montcalm, 43, 45
Müller, Captain von, 57

Nelson, Lord, Royal Naval traditions of, 2, 4, 24, 49, 61
Newcastle, H.M.S., 43, 45
North Wales, S.S., 76
Nürnberg, 4, 54, 56, 62–3; CORONEL: 7; sinks *Monmouth*, 17–18, 55.— Movements after Coronel, 53; at Más-a-Fuera, 68; rounds the Horn, 85; at Picton Island, 96; moves to attack Port Stanley, 97, 99–100; FALKLAND ISLANDS, 122, 149, 156, 164–5; turns eastward, 106; attempts to escape, 137–41; engages *Kent*, 141–2; on fire, 142; speed

drops, 142–3; completely wrecked, and sinks, 143–6

Orama, armed merchantman, 45, 48, 50, 51, 156, 167
Otranto, armed merchant cruiser, 3, 5, 27, 33, 45, 48, 70; under Cradock's command, 2; CORONEL: 6–8, 54; departs unscathed, 11.—Heads for Magellan Straits, 16, 20–1

Palma, 82
Penas Gulf: *Canopus* enters, 20; East Asiatic Squadron in, 81; the squadron leaves, 85
Pernambuco, 80, 82
Pathfinder, H.M.S., 39
Pfulf, Lieutenant, 132
Phillimore, Captain (H.M.S. *Inflexible*), 131, 132
Pichert, Paymaster-Lieutenant, 145
Picton Island, East Asiatic Squadron at, 94–7
Pochhammer, Commander Hans, 132, 135, 136
Port Pleasant, approached by German colliers, 108
Port Stanley (Falkland Islands), 21, 92, 93; reported as abandoned, 76–7; coal stocks at, 91; guarded by *Canopus*, 94; von Spee plans to attack, 96–7; East Asiatic Squadron moves to attack, 97–101; Admiral Sturdee's forces in, 102–5; British warships return to, 158–9
Princess Royal, H.M.S., 45
Prinz Eitel Friedrich, 51, 63, 68, 72
Punta Arenas, 61, 65, 76

Queen Adelaide Archipelago, 21
Raeder, Captain (later Admiral), 135, 163
Ramses, collier, 76, 80
Rasch, Chief Warrant Officer, 145
Richmond, Captain (later Admiral) Herbert, 36

Sacramento, S.S. 63–4, 68, 71, 72
Samoa: German base in, 32; von Spee's descent upon, 59–60
San Quentin Sound, East Asiatic Squadron in, 76, 78
Santa Elena, Port, German agency at, 80, 83, 91–3, 95
Santa Isabel, 63, 68, 80, 96, 108, 157

Schack, Sub-Lieutenant, 146
Scharnhorst (von Spee's Flagship), 3,
20, 27, 32–3, 57, 62–3, 79, 92, 103;
CORONEL: 6–9, 11, 53, 56; engaged
by *Glasgow*, 16; engages *Good Hope*,
54; slightly damaged, 55.—Range of
her guns, 28; movements after
Coronel, 53; at Más-a-Fuera, 68;
ammunition used at Coronel, 71;
rounds the Horn, 85; moves to
attack Port Stanley, 106; FALKLAND
ISLANDS: 162–4; accepts action, 110;
on fire, 114, 117, 123–8; engaged by
Invincible and *Inflexible*, 118; sinks,
118–19, 128
Schenk, Dr, 81–3, 89
Schönberg, Captain von (*Nürnberg*),
17–18, 53, 62, 96, 105, 142–5, 153,
168
Schultze, Captain von, 101, 125
Seydlitz, battleship, 81
Seydlitz, collier, 76, 80, 96, 108, 157
Singapore, 32
Smythe Channel, 21
Spee, Admiral Graf von, 3, 4, 9, 21,
27, 33, 35, 39, 44, 45, 49, 162, 168;
CORONEL: orders full steam, 6; keeps
distance from British force, 7;
suspects torpedo attack, 13; letter
on the battle, 53–6.—British uncertainty on his whereabouts, 50–1;
his 'Fleet in Being' concept, 57–9;
his descent upon Samoa, 59–60;
attacks Tahiti, 60; near Easter
Island, 60; at Más-a-Fuera, 60–1;
his ships, 62–4; at Valparaiso, 64–7;
help from Naval Staff, 69–70; uncertain of whereabouts of British
forces, 70; desires to dash for home,
72–3; orders coal and provisions,
73–4; movements of British forces
reported to, 77; and Britain's power,
77–8; considers capturing Falkland
Islands, 78–9, 91; and coaling
problems, 79–81, 89; and Dr
Schenk's news, 81–4; awarded Iron
Cross, 84; takes his squadron round
the Horn, 85–94; fails to receive
intelligence, 94–5; considers attacking Port Stanley, 96–7; orders attack
97; FALKLAND ISLANDS: orders his
ships not to accept action, 100, 106;
orders light cruisers to escape, 110,
122; flies southwards, 112–13, 123–

4; signals *Gneisenau* to escape, 118,
128; closes the range, 125; his tactics
criticized, 165
Spee, Sub-Lieutenant Graf von, 145–6
Stoddart, Admiral, 29, 34, 110, 136,
166
Sturdee, Vice-Admiral Sir Frederick
Doveton, 37, 94; his command and
objective, 46–7; and Lord Fisher,
48; moves his squadron south, 49–
50; uncertain of enemy position, 51;
receives news of von Spee's squadron, 103; FALKLAND ISLANDS: recalls
Kent, 106; orders 'General Chase',
107; orders reduction of speed, 108;
and German gunnery, 114; changes
course, 115; orders battle-cruisers
to turn to port, 117; and *Scharnhorst*'s end, 119; and closure of the
range, 125 ; message to commander
of *Gneisenau*, 136 ; orders chase of
Dresden, 156; and the German
transport vessels, 157; turns back
towards Falklands, 158–9; orders
repairs, 159; conduct of battle
criticized, 161–4

Tahiti, von Spee sinks gunboat in
Papeete harbour, 59–60
Teneriffe, 82
Tierra del Fuego, 93
Tirpitz, Grand Admiral von, 78
Titania, 63–4, 68, 75, 79
Tsingtao: German base at, 32; fall
of, 74

Ushuaia, British telegraphic installation at, 95

Valentine, S.S., 68, 69, 71, 72, 75
Vallenar Bay, 76
Valparaiso, von Spee at, 64–7
Verner, Lieut-Commander Rudolph,
49, 102, 106, 109–10, 111, 113, 115,
117, 118, 126, 130, 168
Von der Tann, 81

Warrior, H.M.S., 163
Weymouth, H.M.S., 43
Wilshin, Engineer-Commander, 5